PRAISE FOR BEGINNER'S MIND

"Quirky, wise, fierce, impossibly creative, Miss D is the fourth-grade teacher we all wish we had. Risk-taking and grace-under-pressure are among the lessons she teaches her students in a hardscrabble shipyard town, sometimes at great cost. M.B. McLatchey has repaid the gift in full, adding Miss D to that pantheon of teachers we never forget, who change our lives forever – for the better. A must-read for every parent and teacher."

– Kevin McIntosh, *Class Dismissed*

"Einstein said he loved talking to young children because they hadn't yet been brainwashed by education. In the sciences, it is so important to look at nature with an open mind, without preconceived notions and biases. M.B. McLatchey captures all of this in *Beginner's Mind*, revealing its secrets to the reader through the innocent eyes of a remarkable fourth grader. Read this book and re-open your mind."

– Robert Fleck, PhD, Emeritus Professor of Physics & Astronomy, Art History as Science History from the Paleolithic to the Present

"M.B. McLatchey's readers encounter a visionary in this memoir about her fourth-grade classroom, a place where the dictionary becomes a 'Sanctuary,' where students leave space at the top of their papers for Big Ideas, and where the Busy People's constant motion isn't considered a nuisance but made useful instead. The teacher, Miss D, insists that her students learn to trust themselves in a world where authority offers little room for singularity. "Don't look back," she urges us, because every day is another chance to choose how you want to live your life. *Beginner's Mind* has galvanized my teaching."

– Frankie Rollins, *The Grief Manuscript*

BEGINNER'S MIND

From Shipyard to Harvard Yard:
Embracing Endless Possibilities

M.B. McLatchey

Regal House Publishing

Published by
Regal House Publishing, LLC
Raleigh, NC 27612
All rights reserved

ISBN -13 (paperback): 9781646030682
ISBN -13 (epub): 9781646030934
Library of Congress Control Number: 2020940210

All efforts were made to determine the copyright holders and obtain their
permissions in any circumstance where copyrighted material was used.
The publisher apologizes if any errors were made during this process, or
if any omissions occurred. If noted, please contact the publisher and all
efforts will be made to incorporate permissions in future editions.

Interior and cover design by Lafayette & Greene
lafayetteandgreene.com
Cover images © by andrey_l/Shutterstock
Author photo credit: Daryl R. LaBello

Regal House Publishing, LLC
https://regalhousepublishing.com

The obituary of Katherine Dunning from *The Boston Globe*. © 1992
Boston Globe Media Partners. All rights
reserved. Used under license.

Printed in the United States of America

For Miss D

and for that generation of Misses in our schools that prized immeasurable goals in a place of measured outcomes.

CONTENTS

AUTHOR'S NOTE:

According to my fourth-grade report card, the year was 1967. The date would be written across its cover in my teacher's hand as plain, undisputable fact:

Promotion to Grade 5, Summa Cum Laude, 1966–1967

But the truth is that it was a suddenly timeless period in a shipbuilding town south of Boston. Population: Portuguese, Irish, Italian, Greek—and, in a lingering season of old dying out and young moving in, of freshly painted houses and new, mysterious gardens—Pakistani and Lebanese.

The town was North Weymouth, Massachusetts, where generations of fathers and sons would learn their trades at The Yard—the Quincy Fore River Shipyard. For the men of North Weymouth—welders, electricians, pipefitters, and plumbers; apprentices, journeymen, and masters—The Yard would be their training ground in the value of a dollar and in the meaning of words like loyalty, brotherhood, family, God, and love.

But for the teacher of their children—Katherine Arthur Dunning, *Miss D* to her students—the training ground would be the classroom. What follows is a series of slides in split screen. Blended with the report of a watchful ten-year-old in pigtails are the author's observations and reflections—decades later—on the transformative power of that year, and of that teacher and mentor, in a new world called Room 20.

Apart from Miss D, actual names and identities are not presented here. Where dialogue and scenes occur, they are recaptured exactly as they were at the time: as seedling for far reaching ideas—as a spark for the beginner's mind.

In the beginner's mind there are many possibilities, but in the expert's mind there are few.

- Shunryu Suzuki

PART I

Fall

FIRST LAWS

Always my steady hand instead of his. The level spoon; the crystals' lava pool. The creamy crest of chicory foam. The nutty steam. His nod that links me to the coffee's warmth. We are all ritual. At ten years old, I know my place and I know what talk looks like here. In this early morning stillness, my father and I move with a laser-sharp sureness around the outlines of things—predawn more like a lingering night. We tell the time according to the laws of this shipyard town. Outside, the still, black air of gulls in hiding; the static charge of church bells in suspension; the caw of a neighbor's coughing; the town slowly waking. Inside, the scent of dairy: boiled eggs and mayonnaise.

I fold fresh sandwiches into his metal pail. I fill his thermos, a layer of reflective glass guiding my steamy black pour; seal it and lay it in the pail's dome top; fasten the thermos arm. I worry about the rust. From my school, a chocolate bar I tuck inside, a small surprise for him—rations like small devotions intended, later, at the Yard, to keep him alert and on guard. As if to tap them out, I dust the dents with my rag.

We are right on time. The kitchen's window glass mutates from coal black to a wet, woolen gray, and we hear the call of the Shipyard's flexing cranes. When my father opens the kitchen door wide and stands in the threshold—half leaving, half frozen midstride—we take it in: the fragrance of pita bread rising a block away; the briny scent of low tide. Then, the blast of cold morning air when he leaves for his day. The veil of ocean mist melting on the kitchen windowpane when I wave goodbye.

When the Shipyard's first horn blows, we will check our mental lists. We will picture slim men in hard hats, heads bowed, lunch pails in hand, passing through the Yard's heavy gate—and we will summon ourselves. This is our village dance.

This morning I am excited by the dance. I am wearing my new school dress—a black-and-white plaid princess dress with a Peter Pan collar and a velvet bow at the top. Against my mother's wish, I am wearing it unwashed: fresh off the store hanger, starched and new, in a way that it will never be new again. I spin to make its hem parachute.

The Shipyard's horn: seven a.m.

My brothers have already established a steady stride ahead of me. I charter my course to school, fixing my eyes on their backs. There is no way I could know yet what it will mean to trust my own instincts or to cut my own path.

October, 1973

I had meant to write sooner, but things have been so hectic! In response to your last letter, let me say this: you can never be medium and I guess I wouldn't want you to be even if it spared you pain.

You can be gloriously alone on a mountaintop, but in the valleys you walk with mankind.

Love always,

Miss D

RIGHT NOTES

Long before we hear it, we feel it. The treble hum of one boy, then another, intoning the notes of an a cappella that is winding its way down the long sheeny hall toward us. The confident girls brush the cantors away. They sing their own rondo: a circle of chatter about girlfriends stealing girlfriends, about sleepovers, about the sensual unknown of after-school. In a performance that is part Carol Channing, part Hepburn, the lead boy presses his lips together and mimics the long, muffled moan of a distant chant. Primping unruly and invisible curls, he weaves his way among us, until at last he leads his congregation in singing some of the Ordinary—the Sanctus and the Agnes Dei.

Of course, he is mocking her. And yet, his insolence requires such study of her pulse, her every note, it's difficult to see him as condemned. He takes us to her like a divining rod. With each approach, softer and softer, we hear the Sanctus—or is it the Agnes Dei?—until, with resounding confidence, the Sanctus reigns. By the time we reach the doorway to her classroom, we know how her piece goes. At the threshold to Room 20, in a pitch that Johnson Public Elementary School would rightly characterize as religious, we are humming the right notes.

It is our third week of school in the fourth grade. She is the only teacher who does not escort us from the playground to the classroom. "You know your way back," she will say with a thermal hug, and we know what she means, but not really. There are terms here, but they are so encoded, apparently too precious to iterate. It is as if the most perfunctory elements of our lives—leaving and returning—will now require from us a new vigilance, a wakefulness. Parents and federal laws aside, coming back will require—oddly enough—an exercise of our will.

It is an exercise that we let ourselves fail. With each return, we glance through the glass-paneled doors of the other classrooms. We envy the fifth-grade class whose teacher has so creatively drawn up her rules of conduct in the form of the Bill of Rights—a giant brown paper scroll, unrolled for all to read. For a look of authenticity, she has even burned the scroll's edges and painted in shimmering gold glitter the numbered Amendments—laws like the comfortable half-truths of school that we can hardly remember now.

With each return, there is always this sideways glance, the nostalgia for dioramas: for the promising cool of oily-blue rivers in shoeboxes, for the tedium of Colonial-day chores made bearable under sticker-star skies and amid towers of Nabisco Shredded Wheat, for the parade of miniature clay resisters buckled over by the weight of their clay berets before they can reach the Bastille.

We long for the cycles of seedlings in Dixie cups, for the classroom door covered in Christmas paper as if to reveal a perfect package—a Toyland of busy, smiling learners. We envy their self-containment, their ease with platitudes.

By contrast, our classroom door is always open, an endless welcome—or, as we come to imagine it, an endless acquittal for our quiet betrayals. But it is never an easy acquittal. From the farthest end of the hallway, we can read her puzzling greeting. Gothic letters trimmed in gold leaf, letters sized to the width of our classroom door, and each one filled in with stories and faces and figures from an Old World. And the message on the classroom door, so alarming:

GO AWAY!

MAPS INSIDE

We literally do not know if we are coming or going, except that there are indeed maps inside—navigational charts primarily, but also the quaint Countries and Industries maps with sheep eternally grazing in ranges eternally lush and green. On every desk, a compass, and between the rows of desks: atlases, feathered hats, and rolls of paper spilling from boxes. On the walls above the blackboard: the faces of adventurers—*noble exiles*, she calls them.

COLUMBUS, COPERNICUS,
MOSES, GANDHI,
GALILEO, GAUGUIN, ODYSSEUS

And beneath Odysseus's cold black eyes and his pouting homesick mouth is the directive:

BE INSPIRED

But our stomachs are still registering Odysseus's homesickness, and we find ourselves standing still as if to discern which is moving. Us? Or like a ship leaving port—this room? We stare back at Odysseus in an effort to keep him at his lonely post, ourselves on land. We steady ourselves. The groundskeeper putters below and a scent of sulfur stirs the maps on the wall. We are going away. Or else we are coming home.

November, 1975

Please don't study too hard or be too impressed by the intellectualism surrounding you. You! Wish I could find that French dictionary. There is an idiom that says what I want to say perfectly.

Your loving teacher and student,

D

THE RESISTANCE

There is an enormous dictionary in our classroom—so massive that, on every turn of the page, it threatens to crush to a glittering dust the folding card table that supports it. Our teacher has crossed out the word *Dictionary* and written instead, in beautiful Palmer script, the word *Sanctuary*. Webster's *Sanctuary*. On the floor is a throw carpet charting Marco Polo's long dream—a broken line stitched through the Bay of Bengal and the South China Sea. In the same corner, in marine blues and crushed-velvet reds are overstuffed pillow chairs.

In spite of the invitation that we sense from all the props, we visit the *Sanctuary* less often than we should—and not one of us ever looks up the word *inspire*. But, if inspiration means *to breathe life into*, then it is literally Miss D's breathing that draws us back each day. Swept up in the progress of her own drone hum, she absently smiles at us as we drift in, then mimes her directions to us: her arms breaststroking through an invisible ocean:

Make room for song.

Palms down, then open and rising:

Raise up your voices.

We know these gestures as phrases because they are tacked to the bulletin board for DAILY ANNOUNCEMENTS. Where other teachers have posted the daily news, our teacher has hung a giant poster-board musical staff on which she strings daily reflections like musical notes. Instead of today's date and weather and a calendar of school events hanging on our bulletin board, we find large thoughts strung across her musical staff like lyrics to songs that we do not know yet:

No man is an island

or

I think, therefore I am!

On occasion, as it happened during one Lenten-gray February in A major, whole months could pass in a single, unwavering scale. For a whole month, we would look toward the DAILY ANNOUNCEMENTS board and see the same message in the same climbing scale:

_____the right notes_____
_____it helps each of us sing_____
_____ at the same time _____
__ If we sing the same notes _____

It takes us several weeks to recognize that there will be no such thing as Daily Announcements, and that this will be information that we will have to gather elsewhere. During recess, or amid the thrill of fire drills, we skulk about like spies among our peers. We become experts at piecing together the most ordinary bits of information: "Third bell means fourth-grade recess, right?" "The fourth-graders are going to the Christmas play today, right?" "Report cards come out this week, right?" Day by day, the very details that we have been taught to regard as the most critical parts of our lives since we entered the public school system will eventually come to be regarded by us as the most dispensable and inconsequential details of our lives. After a while, we will lose interest altogether in these details. We will stop asking the easy questions. And yet, this will not be an easy transformation. As with all of the metamorphoses that we would experience in Miss D's class, we do not give up our learned habits, our learned values, without resistance.

Resistance, for John G. Ashe, would mean requiring a working clock in our classroom. Since our first day in the fourth grade, John G. Ashe has politely informed Miss D that the clock in our classroom has stopped. Each morning, as we line up for outdoor recess, John G. Ashe pauses in front of Miss D and points to the clock above our classroom door and then demurely informs her, "Excuse me, Miss D, but our clock is broken."

For the first few days, Miss D glances up where John G. Ashe is pointing and then hugs him and thanks him for his "eagle eye." Recess after recess, it becomes clear to us that John G. Ashe is going to continue telling Miss D that our clock is not working; and recess after recess, it becomes clear that Miss D has no intention of fixing it. After a while, John G. Ashe simply points his long, slender finger, or tips his head toward the silent and inert clock; each time he does this, Miss D offers the same appreciative hug to him.

Several recesses later, several bright mornings and gray afternoons later, several weeks of wet leaves and several footpaths through a snowy playground later, Miss D would finally lean toward John G. Ashe and toward our single-file line to announce, "Let's not worry about that beast of a clock, children. I prefer the ticking of your hearts! Don't you?"

We are so surprised by the idea that Miss D has been apparently keeping time by the beating of our hearts—and we are perhaps so oddly flattered by the idea as well—that not one of us questions her. Glen Rooney, the smartest boy in our class, even announces that he thinks we should get through our math lessons much faster this way, since his heart has a pretty rapid beat. But for John G. Ashe and for a majority of us who have come up through our first three grades as stellar students, this is witchcraft, or voodoo, or unusual timekeeping at best.

We are not like other fourth-graders, and we know this. While our peers flourish in the transparency of a day's scheduled tasks, we grow in the cool shade of musical signature patterns: big ideas tacked onto an oversized musical staff that tell us—not how to exit for fire drills, not when to eat our lunches, not when to end our school day—but how to live. While others fall into a kind of communal march through the stages of a school day—lessons, recess, and final lessons—we move from math to reading to recess to art by observing entirely different laws of time.

We tell time according to the rhythms of our own beating hearts. We tell time according to the slightly impatient tapping of Miss D's hand on her lap as we linger too long over a word problem. We tell time by the symphonies of light that penetrate our row of windows and that play across our floor and walls: the sacral gold hues of late morning like saints casting off their halos; the florescent and ambivalent gray of midday; and always the same metallic sliver of skylight that stretches itself across our desks to announce the day's final dismissal.

We feel the shift away from a material world toward an interior world, away from the secular in favor of the spiritual, away from the literal in favor of metaphor. And, as if already aware of the casualties that can accompany shifts like this— and as seasoned offspring of the public school system—we long for our old routines. We yearn for an hour hand that moves and we grieve the loss of a kind of happy captivity when our days, our goals, our gods were all concepts drawn up for us by our teacher, or by the principal, or by our parents—by anyone but us.

August 1976

Human relationships are so fragile, and sometimes the world will get in the way and we won't be able to find each other at all and we'll both feel cheated and lost. Oh, darling, I don't think time ever heals. You just become used to living with the wound.

Your loving teacher and pupil,

Miss D

Isms

As if she is suffering from a terrible toothache, Mary Wiles has wrapped her woolen scarf around her oval face. Head bent, shoulders rising and falling in silent gasps, she is determined to finish her worksheet. From one row over, we can see the rivers of ink coursing down her paper and making a soggy bank at her right hand. She wraps and rewraps her scarf until it is apparent that it is not her own ache, but Sara's bruised and swollen legs that she is bandaging.

Sara's sobbing comes in little fits now through the thick door. A cuckoo out of sync and out of key, she bleats out her objections: *No. She does not want to go to the nurse's office. No. She does not want to show the nurse. No. She does not want everything better. No. No.*

Sara and Miss D are in Camelot, the stairwell just outside our classroom, the stairwell that we and the other second-floor classrooms use for fire drills. Weeks ago, after several days of King Arthur, we changed the EXIT sign above the door to EXETER as a surprise for Miss D.

"Children!" Miss D shouted, not taking her eyes off the new sign, "This is no longer a way out. It is now a way *in.*"

Shortly after, Exeter became our passageway—not to fire drills—but to an ideal place, a place that we could go to on any day, at any time. During math lesson, in the middle of language arts, in the midst of a peer's recitation, any one of us might rise from his seat and wander in to feel time stop, to be alone, to feel the quiet, to walk away, to feel the train of joy in breaking rules, to hear one's own heart beat—and after a while, to miss the others, to want the others.

Next to the door is a throne on wheels: Miss D's chair draped with a checkered print—remainder from an Easter dress that Mary Gillis donated, and for which act of charity her parents punished her for weeks. For a ceremonial feel: green and white pompoms retrieved from someone's bicycle, and hung from the arms. On birthdays, and on composition days, any one of us is allowed to wheel the throne through Exeter and into Camelot. Time and time again, Nicholas Kastinopoulos will plant himself in the throne during our writing hour; notebook and pencil in hand, he will tip his head back in thought and wait for the muses to descend upon him. When Bailey Arnold will not stop sniffling, Sabrina Kaslov will retreat to the throne for a quiet read. And when John G. Ashe becomes suddenly impatient with the fourth grade in general, he will huff off to the throne for what Miss D calls "his spell in the catbird seat."

Today, however, the throne stares back at us: abandoned, unconsulted. We picture the two of them, Miss D and Sara, sitting on the cold concrete stairs in Camelot and everything seems out of order—the earth off its axis.

֎

This is "isms" month, the month when each of us brings in a word that ends in *ism*, what Miss D calls a *verbum*—a word among words. For most of us, the choice of word has nothing to do with meaning, although Miss D assures us that *meanings will come, meanings will come.*

We flip through the *Sanctuary*, reading each word from right to left, and pouncing on the first *–ism* we find. We scribble down the root word as an afterthought. On Presentation Day, we make the words our own. We copy our words onto brightly colored placards; we take turns holding our words in front of the class; we say our words to the class and hear the class say them back; we say the word in a sentence of our own making; and then—the most exciting part—we climb a ladder and hang the word above the blackboard.

Today, against the sound of Sara's desperate crying, we sit helpless and helplessly alone in our seats. Some of us are scanning the room as if to find a word for what is happening:

Ac-tiv-ism

Rac-ism

Others are quietly weeping. Like a virus, Sara's garbled lament is spreading through the classroom.

Pat-ri-ot-ism

Os-trac-ism

Mag-net-ism

We struggle to remember the sentences that the words belong in.

Last week, during science, one of the boys in the class showed us how magnets too close to one another will push each other away. We gasped a collective gasp to see how pull became push so suddenly, how at precisely the point where we thought that the magnets would grasp one another and fall into one another's magnetic orbits—instead they spun away from one another. Miss D said that sometimes it was the same with people too.

Against the muffled din of Sara's spasmodic cries, that moment seems to come back to us now, that moment that we saw during show-and-tell, not as science, but as an inexplicable moment when like things rejected one another.

In the first seat of the row closest to Exeter, Glen Rooney is lifting the visor to his astronaut's helmet. The helmet was a gift from Miss D after Glen announced to her one day his dream of orbiting the earth. On a typical day, he dons the helmet from morning arrival until afternoon dismissal—retiring it to the top of his desk only for recess, but always wearing it for fire drills. During whole-class lessons, he peers through the helmet's plastic shield while he reads Miss D's lips as she guides us at the blackboard, or as she shuttles us through the sentences of the great Roman orators: Cicero's impassioned speeches parsed into columns of persuasive words like the

23

concrete columns of the Roman Republic. During writing and reading hours, Glen sits at his desk hovering over word problems or over his science text as if he is hovering over the earth's arc—his only air supply coming from his deco-style, laminated desk: his port, his dream base.

Today, however, Glen Rooney is leaving his port: He has lifted his visor, and is wiping his nose and gasping for air. He seems to be breathing some noxious gas. A few of the motherly girls surround Glen, tell him to go back inside, back under his hood, and not to cry. Somehow, we need him to do as they say. If Glen stops breathing, surely we all will.

&

Org-an-ism

In spite of Miss D's and Sara's absence, Sabrina Kaslov is determined to present her word. It is after morning songs, after math lesson, and it is her turn. She is the prettiest girl in the class, and she is accustomed to performing on queue. She stands before us, and with an affected British accent, she reads the definition that she has copied directly out of the *Sanctuary*:

ORGAN-ISM: ... the whole as well as the parts, and the relations of the parts to the whole ....

None of us are listening. Definitions, we have learned by now, are hardly meanings. Definitions are what Miss D calls, *small attempts at meanings.* They are too tentative, too lacking in the context of a life truly lived. They are—and this Miss D says with her arms swinging through the air—*too sweeping.* Although Miss D has gone, we can feel the lasting breeze of her swinging arms. What we want is Sabrina's sentence—her word in a real context, the life truly lived.

But, Sabrina has clearly rehearsed something more polished. In addition to her comprehensive list of meanings for the word, she offers a catalogue of examples. Organism as ecosystem, organism as biosystem, organism as governmental system. She seems to be speaking in tongue and yet, none of us are moved.

For a visual, she holds up a photo-enlarged mushroom—a fungus, she tells us, and not nature gone wrong. *Organism par excellence.* She offers an accent aigu on the word *excellence.* She reads, from a powder-blue note card, words that she has copied verbatim from the *Sanctuary:*

fungus: a spongy growth, like proud flesh formed in a wound

We are tired and distracted, and we are disgusted by her image. But Miss D has returned to the classroom and is already on her feet. She is singing, "Oh! Oh! Oh! Children! Did you hear that?" And she is writing Sabrina's horrid description on the board:

Like proud flesh formed in a wound

And Miss D is singing,

"Science and poetry! Poetry and science!

See how we need one another?"

We do see it.

Although Miss D has returned, Sara's seat is empty. We feel Sara's absence like the absence of exact meaning, like a story too awful for language to hold—but that perhaps science, or medicine, or a school nurse's care might heal. We feel the desperate beating heart in Sabrina's analogy—and in all analogies.

Like proud flesh formed in a wound.

We see the precision of science in the face of human suffering, and we feel the lightness that comes with that precision. And, we know we won't be graded on this—not today at least.

February, 1977

Being young is so torturously difficult. It breaks my heart. But, never take the easy course, darling, the plusher path because it's plush. Keep on questioning, doubting, and being frustrated, if you must, but never lose your sense of wonder, and above all, "through thick and thin, include me in."

Ever lovingly,

Miss D

A Good and Simple Meal

The Shipyard's tired trombone. We imagine the morning shift falling in, and we shift in our seats accordingly. Like trained monastics, we look up from our morning lessons, our Matins, expecting John Paul Ambrose III. He is later than usual.

Four out of five mornings, he arrives after the second horn, offering apologies: ten-car pileups, bus collisions; the bridge was up and a Royal fleet passed under it—their linen sails seemed to touch the soles of my feet. Fires, fallen limbs, occasional fatalities. Though we want his fantastic stories, we know better. We have seen John Paul Ambrose III with his mother, now and then, at the corner store. We have heard her slurring speech, watched her struggling to count her change, fighting to stay still, straddling to keep from falling over as if her earth were on a different axis than his and ours. And John Paul Ambrose III, standing so stiff beside her as if to keep her upright, and the grocer's suspended light bulbs bathing his silky, bowed head in a shimmering light.

Most of us have had our turn in the whiskey-damp air of this shipyard town: mothers suddenly sour-breathed and graceless; and the good fathers, the ones who come home with their paychecks, the ones who take their drink at home. Most of us have had our turn in those days without prospect, and so the shame on the face of John Paul Ambrose III is our shame as well.

Our town was a town between bridges, yet so often there seemed to be no way out. When Mary Wiles put it that way, or something like that, Miss D shook her head hard and

27

hollered at her, "High Art, Mary! High Art!" Miss D hated self-pity. Self-pity, she said, is a common man's art, and her students in Room 20 will be making high art this year.

The distance from Johnson Elementary School in North Weymouth to Harvard University in Cambridge was a fairly direct route of about fifteen miles. Forever standing between those two points, however—as if to intercept certain life ambitions—were the colossal cranes of the Quincy Fore River Shipyard. Like cathedrals that generations of men from the surrounding towns had built, the Shipyard's cranes pierced the sky and towered above behemoth ships below them. And like medieval cathedrals, the cranes and ships became points of destination in themselves.

In the early morning hours and then again in the late afternoons, in a changing of shifts that looked more like the rotation of pilgrims, our fathers and grandfathers make their tired treks over the bridge going to and from the Shipyard. When the morning air is cold and clear, we hear the gigantic cranes flex, and swerve, and lean, and yaw as we dress for school or as we linger over our toast and tea.

The history of the Quincy Shipyard and of the Fore River Bridge that guarded its entrance was *our* history. A proud leader in the U.S. shipbuilding industry with a massive gantry crane that could be seen for miles, it was *our* home field. We marked the change in seasons according to the building phases of freighters and tankers. We knew the war was over when the Yard grew quiet. Our surnames were inscribed into the Shipyard's payroll book and our initials were etched into the bridge's iron railings: *MB was here,* or *TM loves MG,* and, of course, *Kilroy was here.*

In the spring, when the bridge hoists itself up to let a string of boats pass under it, we pour out of our stopped cars and fight for a spot to lean over the bridge's railings and watch the parade of barges, sailboats, and scows below. In the winter, when the bridge's steel and lattice floor ices up, our cars careen into the bridge's iron curb like seals on their bellies. And on hot afternoons after school, on a dare from their peers, our brothers jump from ledges beneath the bridge, risking their lives as they catapult into the water below. From the back seats of our cars, we see them leap into the murky depths and our hearts leap too with fear and horror—and pride.

As if she has never heard of these hallowed places, Miss D presents us not with field trips to the Shipyard or to local industries, but with a map of the universe; not with creative lessons about the great Commonwealth of Massachusetts, but with instructions on how to plot stars from our bedroom windows at night.

When in doubt, look up, she tells us.

We take her advice to mean that for answers we should look toward the stars, or toward our various gods, and we notice that she does not say *look around*. Her lessons all but forbid us from looking around; all but prohibit us from re-lying upon the familiar references in our lives for answers. Answers, in fact, are the last thing that Miss D seems to want from us.

What she seems to want from us is something immea-surable in a place of measured outcomes—a new way of behaving that, as best as we can tell, our first-grade teacher, second-grade teacher, and third-grade teacher at Johnson Elementary have already classified as *acting out* and cause for a trip to the principal's office. As much as we will remember about this year, we will not remember one of us ever being sent to the principal's office.

The door to Exeter is propped open so that John Paul Am-brose III can slip in from the back of the school, unaffected and unnoticed by Miss Rose in the school's front office with her massive tome filled with notes and grids titled Tardy,

Absent, Sick. When John Paul Ambrose III does arrive, his face is damp and flushed, his eyes dark and blank, his pants and shirt clinging to his narrow frame.

Miss D has set out his breakfast: a banana-nut muffin and a bottle of apple juice. Next to this, a packet of papers rolled up and tied in purple ribbon—this morning's worksheets prepared for him, as one might prepare a judge's morning schedule.

He slouches toward his morning meal and begins to eat without looking up, without looking at any of us. But we are all looking at him. Miss D has told us again and again that, when he does come, our Savior will wear a beggar's clothes, and that it is *we* who should be ready for *him*, not he for us. We have finished our morning lessons, and we gaze at John Paul Ambrose III as if we are expecting a speech or a vision or some sign from him.

The smell of banana and nut winds through our classroom. It is a good morning for our Savior: no tardy slip, no detention, and a good and simple meal.

June, 1978

Just finished reading about Gandhi's life again. I read it once a decade to remind myself which warriors God seems to love best. Don't worry, darling, it's not who you might think.

Ever yours,

Miss D

THE WARRIOR RACE

Amid streamers in black and orange, amid toothless jack-o-lanterns and the scent of hay and hops, we move through our classroom like we have never moved through a classroom before. Everywhere in Room 20, there is an aspect of play that our teacher is so at ease with we assume it is all a grand joke: pencils neatly stored in the box labeled Scissors; paper clips in the box marked Milk Money. Nearly everything about our classroom testifies to Miss D's apparent disinterest in rules of order that we have come to rely upon. Nearly everything about her way with us reminds us of her quiet check on the current orthodoxy.

As much as we might stretch by allying ourselves to Miss D, instead we cling to our habits of thinking the way that theologians once clung to a flawed model of the universe. And, like good theologians, we set out to prove the fallacies in Miss D's worldview. We do this by constantly testing Miss D. We misbehave.

Time and again, we take advantage of Miss D's apparent lack of classroom management. When Miss D asks us to please take out our pencils for a test that the state of Massachusetts wants us to take, Bailey Arnold leaps to his feet, dashes to the storage closet at the back of the classroom, and then distributes pairs of scissors to the class. The flourish of clapping scissor hands that drowns out the principal's testing instructions over the loudspeaker in our classroom triggers an eruption of laughter that mounts and mounts—until we notice that Miss D is laughing too. There, at her desk, she is doubled over, hands clapping and laughing so hard that she can barely manage to speak.

But she does speak: "O children! We are a symphony of scissors!"

Apparently surprised and disappointed by Miss D's collaboration in his masterpiece of misbehaving, Bailey Arnold angrily collects our scissors, insists that we are all ridiculous, settles himself into his seat, and begins reviewing the test on his desk. The rest of us bow our heads and meekly follow his lead.

From this day forward, Miss D will remember and even celebrate Bailey Arnold's joke. Our pencils will remain stored in the box labeled Scissors, and she will begin our composition lessons not with the usual announcement, but with a call to battle. "Take out your weapons!" Miss D will shout to us at the start of Writing Time. Like fledglings falling into line, we will scramble toward the box labeled Scissors for a No. 2 with a good lead tip, while Sabrina Kaslov brandishes her pencil from a velvet sleeve.

Once tucked back into our seats, a hush of deep thoughts will come over us while autumn gusts paste burnt-red leaves to our classroom windows, or while veils of snow whisk by. Bailey Arnold will hunch over his composition notebook like a general dreaming over a battle plan. "A perfect day for battle," Miss D whispers each time to us as she strolls around the classroom, and we bow toward our empty composition sheets and wait for the crippled crawl or the distant howl of our own captive thoughts—not writers, but *warriors*.

October, 1979

As for ghosts from the past, darling, it's "the road not taken"
that haunts.

Ever yours,

D

BLISS BANDITS

All Hallow's Eve. According to Miss D, this is the day when magic is in the air. This, she tells us, is what the early Irish called the betwixt and between time. It is the time of year in October when it is neither fall nor winter—a time of transition, a time of ambiguity, a time of passage. We seem to know what Miss D is talking about.

During the last few weeks we have reenacted customs from the Celtic calendar and we have kept our classroom window shades half-drawn to mark the season of diminishing light. In songs and in play-acting, we have dramatized and sometimes felt shook by the superstitions of the early Irish: foot-stomping parades around the perimeter of our classroom to keep the spirits of mischief away.

In order to gather our wits and to frighten off the ghouls that make our minds muddled, we have propped ourselves up in our seats with lit flashlights under our chins—and *then* we were ready for our math quiz. We have held lavish autumn festivals that on two occasions caused us to miss afternoon recess; and, as if aware of the principal's likely disapproval of our festivities, we have periodically disguised ourselves in ghoulish costumes to avoid his persecution.

This is indeed a betwixt and between time, and like never before, we have come to feel this shift in seasons as somehow a shift in our own lives as well. And, as if to equip us with a language for this transition that we are feeling in our lives, Miss D unveils for us in the Irish language a world of transitions, a life of comings and goings, a language of beginnings and endings. We become masters at the bare essentials: Gaelic phrases for happy and sad, for young and old, for hello and goodbye:

> Conas atá tú?   (How are you?)
> Tá mé go maith.   (I'm doing well.)

After a while, we offer these salutations to one another like blessings, or like code for some shared enterprise. "Conas atá tú?" Sabrina Kaslov calls to Mary Gillis as they file in and out of the girls' bathroom. "Go maith," Mary Gillis volleys back. And the rest of us smile and drop our heads to avoid all the inquiries around us.

Not all of us, however, want these Irish blessings: Bailey Arnold decides to demonstrate his mastery of the Irish language by greeting a fifth-grade teacher in Irish:

> Dia duit!   (God be with you!)

But, the teacher pulls him aside by the ear. With her forefinger and thumb lifting his chin, she asks him in a punishing tone, "Would you like to repeat that?"

As if he suddenly regrets the Irish blessing that he once freely offered her, or as if in some sort of state of grace—we cannot tell which—Bailey Arnold simply closes his lips tight and takes a missed recess instead.

"Éirinn go Brách!" a few of the boys call out to Bailey Arnold as they pass him on their way to recess, and he waves to them, uplifted and oddly ebullient for a boy missing recess.

At Johnson Elementary, we have enjoyed our share of Halloween parties—the cardboard cutouts taped to our row of windows: round and jolly pumpkins, black cats with arched backs, and perfectly drawn bats that say *Boo*; the candy corn and chocolate coins. In the first grade, our substitute teacher even came to school in a Halloween costume: a smiling, but oddly tragic, Sleeping Beauty. For the rest of the year, Mary Gillis prayed that the substitute teacher might be saved from her apparent sleepwalking, that she might be saved from her life without a prince. "Just one kiss," Mary kept reminding us. "It takes just one kiss."

In Miss D's class, however, there are no Sleeping Beauty costumes, no stories of princes who rouse us like lovesick children of some Lady Lazarus, no cardboard cutouts like window dressing to make peace with the principal and our parents outside. For costumes in Miss D's class there are only horrible rubber masks—and these are reserved for warding off what Miss D calls The Bliss Bandits.

"Oh, they're out there, children," Miss D would say to us. "They're out there."

As we file past her on our way to recess, or, at the end of the day as we leave her for our trek home, Miss D might pat a few of us on the shoulder and remind us, "Watch out for the Bliss Bandits, darling."

And we do.

If Miss D marks us out, we keep our heads up after that. According to Miss D, the Bliss Bandits could appear in all shapes and sizes, and whether or not they mean to, they will rob us of our bliss in the blink of an eye. Only now we had masks. "This should stop them in their tracks," Miss D puffed one afternoon as she fitted one of the ghoulish masks to the girl with the bruises and belt marks on her legs.

March, 1981

It struck me during the reading in mass this morning—It wasn't the sword, it was Peter the man that was the problem.

Ever lovingly,

D

SWORD POWER

For Reading Hour in Room 20 there are plastic swords—
one for each of us—that Miss D had brought in earlier in
the year during our reading of *Siegfried and the Dragon*. Today,
as she distributes one to each of us, she reminds us of the
power of that sword:

"Where did Siegfried get his strength, children?"

"From the sword!" we answer in unison.

"And where did the sword get its strength, darlings?"

"From Siegfried!"

We are proud that we can volley these answers back at
Miss D with such certainty. For a whole week, we listened
to her read to us during lunchtime about Siegfried's fantastic
and brave adventures. Each time she finished reading, Miss
D would lay the book on her lap like open wings, straighten
her back and smile up at us, and then begin:

"Where did Siegfried get his strength, children?"

After so much practice with this, we could holler back our
answer before we heard the question. By now, we had solved
Miss D's riddle:

The sword is only as strong as the man.

But, it will not be until one surprisingly white morning in
October, a day that Johnson Elementary School might have
called a snow day, when we will hear the harder message in
the tale: The principal's secretary pokes her head into our
classroom and informs us that John G. Ashe should report
to the principal's office immediately because he has bloodied
the nose of a boy on the playground and if she wants to Miss

D can see for herself the trail of blood left in the snow outside. Miss D politely smiles at the secretary and then drops
her face to her lap. When the secretary leaves, Miss D does
not look up from her lap. One of the motherly girls passes
a note to another girl. When Miss D does leave her seat, she
walks heavily toward our supplies closet, pulls out one of the
plastic swords, and brings it to John G. Ashe.

"Try this next time, darling," she tells him.

And, when John G. Ashe throws the sword to the floor,
she picks it up again and tells him in a voice that all of us
can hear:

"I meant for slaying that fiery dragon inside you."

When the secretary's stern voice later calls over the loudspeaker in our classroom for John G. Ashe to report to the
principal's office, he does not move from his seat. As if
feeling all of our eyes upon him, he makes one quick glance
sideways and then drops his head into his folded arms—his
sword tucked under his arms. In Miss D's class, instead of
reading comprehension tests, there are tests on the playground. Instead of trips to the principal's office, there are
plastic swords—swords for accompanying Siegfried on his
journey; swords for slaying our own personal demons.

For the slowest readers and for the worst behavers in
our class, the sword and Miss D's medieval myths seem to
signal to them a way out. By mid-year, with Miss D's encouragement, even Bailey Arnold will choose Dante over
detention: a chance to think about sin and the thrill—Bailey
Arnold tells the rest of us—in making the punishment fit
the sin, like Dante did. "Imagine," Bailey Arnold tells us, "if
we could choose like Dante did, who should go to heaven
and who should go to hell." Compared to the work that we
are expected to do in Miss D's class, a trip to the principal's
office is child's play—at best, a dull game of chess.

May, 1982

How did the practice teaching turn out? Were you scared? I always was. The words of "I Whistle A Happy Tune" helped me most.

Lovingly,

Miss D

A SING-IN

Although we miss the haunted house that we once built from a refrigerator box in third grade, the majority of us have not looked back. We have been marking the days on Miss D's Celtic calendar and feeling more than ever the advent of Halloween as somehow, the advent of a new season in our own lives as well.

And yet, some of us could not help but look back. When Mary Gillis complains that we cannot have a Halloween party without trick-or-treat bags and candy—especially candy corn—an unexpected nostalgia overcomes us. We suddenly share her yearning for the robotic piling up and taking down of seasonal things; we suddenly share her desire for rituals of less consequence.

Apparently, it is a yearning and a nostalgia that even Miss D seems to hear in Mary Gillis's voice. "I suppose so," Miss D says, as if to grant Mary Gillis and the rest of us our candy corn, as if to bow to our God of Conformity. And yet, by now we understand that when Miss D says, "I suppose so," it really means "I don't think so." After brief consideration, we don't think so either.

Candy corn or no candy corn, there are more important seasonal cycles that need our tending to. Perhaps simply because we are ten and eleven years old, or perhaps because we feel Miss D's permission to make our own lives our focus, we feel ourselves in the midst of a maturing of our own: Sabrina Kaslov in her trainer's bra that she does not need yet, but that she adjusts throughout the day with a kind of smug impatience; Nicholas K. in his dead father's oversized shirts that he wears like loose layers of scar tissue over his broken heart; Bailey Arnold, for the first time in his school years not commissioned to the corner of the classroom, but sitting among us and beaming like a hero who has returned from exile.

Dragon slayers. Rites of passage. Seasonal cycles. In Miss D's class, no matter what subjects we are studying, there are always the same lessons in humanity. Like the chorus of an ancient Greek play, we frequently recite these lessons—as we did for *Siegfried and the Dragon*—as part of some play-acting that we have collaboratively invented. After a while these lessons affect us, their maxims stay with us, they ring in our ears long after our chanting is over, and they sometimes even seem to guide us.

This morning, it is as if that chorus, those maxims, *something* is ringing in our ears—something braver than us. What else could explain why, when Miss D stages a sing-in to drown out the principal's morning announcements, we decide to join her.

"I do not subscribe to detaining human beings!" Miss D proclaims to the loud speaker above the door in our classroom; and so, to our horror and delight, with the classroom door open wide, she leads us in a round of song that consumes the principal's voice.

"Oh What a Beautiful Morning." By our fourth week in the fourth grade, we knew it by heart. It was the song we sang on rainy days and on days when Miss D seemed to know more about our lives than we had told her.

This morning, we chime in reflexively. In lilting notes and well-rehearsed parts, our high pitches accompany Miss D's perfectly timed lows. She continues to lead us in song, until the principal has finished this morning's roll of students who will serve after-school detention.

In this unwelcome pause in our song, we see ourselves at

once victorious and condemned. We follow Miss D's lead and stomp our feet twice between verses, ostensibly to keep time with our song, but also—we cannot help but notice—our stomping drowns out the principal's monotone recitation of the names of our peers.

In spite of the fun that we are having, we cannot keep ourselves from imagining the sentencing that awaits us. We cannot keep from watching our open classroom door through which our voices drift like pieces of a play in rough rehearsal—"Oklahoma," we might tell the principal when he arrives, or perhaps a scene from the storming of the Bastille. A tremulous trail of song, our voices echo and hang in the hall like a cloud of noxious gas that, in future days, will stir the other teachers and periodically draw them to our classroom door for a peek inside.

The principal will have to trace the noxious gas past the other open doors, past the other classrooms of children with quiet mouths and quiet minds tucked neatly behind their desks, past Room 15 with its eternally sunlit walls, past the Garden Patch display of Spelling Bees in Room 16, past the first-place ribbons for the third-grade Thespians in Room 18, past Room 19's Roster of Magicians in Math—to us.

Without prompting, a few of the boys in our class get up from their seats in the middle of our singing to put on some of the ghoulish masks that Miss D brought to us. If, as Miss D has told us, these masks will ward off Bliss Bandits; and if, as she claims, the early Irish people wore these masks to chase evil spirits away, perhaps now they will help us against the principal's ire.

As ethereal as Miss D looks to us—floating up and down between our rows of desks and waving her right arm like a conductor of some heavenly chorus—and as much as we feel her invitation to join her on our feet, we also feel the weight of learned habits, of institutional codes that have become the very core of our small consciences. Still, we cannot help but admire and even envy Miss D, so we raise our heavy heads toward her and we stay in our seats and sing in our chains.

These are brazen acts from Room 20 and we know it: to assert that yesterday's misbehavers need not be today's detainees. To flaunt our innocence like Arthur's sterling sword. To take back our kingdom as Arthur did, by releasing a sword from a stone that no one else could release. To trust these occasions as natural law—and not accidents in nature. To see ourselves as part of these natural laws. To trust our sword powers. To trust ourselves. And ultimately, in this makeshift chorus of boy sopranos and girl sopranos led by Miss D's rumbling baritone, to acknowledge what we already know: that the principal is not a man to us, but an idea. And on this particular morning, he is an idea that we dare to challenge.

Certainly the redhead in the second row knows this. She whimpers at the slightest address not only from the principal, but from any adult—even Miss D. And in singing over the principal's announcements some mornings, we seem to caress the belt marks on the backs of her legs. As misplaced a remedy as this seems to us even now, it is as if we realize that this is all we can do for her—and so, most of us sing.

September, 1983

I've thought so much about your last letter. All I can say is I've never been a big fan of the compromise—especially with what matters most.

All my love,

Miss D

RIGHT SPEECH

The most famous speaker in the whole world had a horrible stutter. He was a Greek and smart like Greeks are, and his name was Demokalis."

Demos-the-nes.

No one seems to hear the correction, especially not Nicholas Kastinopoulos, who is wrapping his arm around Tommy Breen's back and sunken shoulders. With every new shot that Nicholas fires, he squeezes Tommy's arm, as if to pull him to his feet.

Since October, Tommy has been *T-T-T-Tommy* to the boys in the fifth grade, not because Tommy stutters like Demosthenes—but because the fifth-grade boys can *make* him stutter. For most of us, it is our first demonstration in how to bring a human being to his knees.

"Who cares about the Greeks?!"

Today, Nicholas K. seems delivered to us.

"I'll show you who cares! I'll show you who cares!"

Until now, we had wondered why we should hear his stories—about his grandfather who dived and dived for sponges; about how they made his father, the strongest man on the boat, go down and down in the dark, black sea to search for his own father.

"I'll show you!"

And now the pieces of his story are coming in a frenzy of bloodied fists. Even over the din of crying girls and chanting boys, we can still hear Nicholas K.:

"… and they put those two men, MY father and HIS father,
    each in his own long box,
    and dropped him! Plop!
    and dropped him!
    into the ocean."

And always, the sweeping motion that Nicholas K. makes with his long, strong arms when he tells this part of the story about the burial at sea of his father and his father's father. And always his broad chest deflated and his beautiful silk shirt, suddenly too large, hangs off his shoulders like a rented toga. And always the pause he requires from us, as if we are seeing the burial ourselves.

At the end of the day, Miss D stays with Nicholas K. He has been called to the principal's office, but Miss D says that Nicholas K. is a noble young Greek, and that it's the office that ought to come here. Although we are eager to go home, the rest of us stay as well. We are in a kind of holding place, a *not-detention*.

In the corner of our classroom, permanently perched on top of a pile of art supplies, and eternally overlooking our clothesline of drying watercolors, is a small wooden figure. *Demosthenes*, Miss D once told us, is the kind of wooden model that artists use when they want to draw the human form. We took her at her word. And in the same way that we do not ask about her car's name—*Eliza*—we did not ask about Demosthenes.

In part, we did not ask because we left it to Nicholas K. With each day, he has established himself as a specialist in all things Greek. His impromptu presentations always a call to our senses: sponges from the shelves of sponge off the coast of Kalymnos; a painted clay urn meant for ashes, but that his mother fills with wine; gold and black stitching on squares of silk, telling stitch by stitch, the stories of Achilles and Hercules—and Demosthenes.

"Tell the part about the pebbles!" we shout.

Nicholas K. has told this part so many times that we can say it with him. Still, he's eager to tell it, and Tommy Breen is eager to grant him this reprieve. And so Nicholas starts,

"No one could have believed that he would become the greatest speaker in Greece—*in the world!* He could hardly say two right words in a row."

"Tell the part about the pebbles," one of the boys interrupts.

"And people made fun of him, and they teased him, and they made him say words that they knew he couldn't say, like p-p-p-pizza and f-f-f–fishcakes."

"Tell about the pebbles!"

"So Demosthenes would fill his mouth with pebbles and practice talking that way, and he would sing songs while he was running, and he would go down to the seashore and shout out whole sentences while the ocean roared and blasted across the rocks."

"Is he still alive?" Mary Wiles asks.

It is a part of the story that we have never heard, so we move in from our various posts around the classroom.

"He gave one speech, then another," Nicholas utters, bowing his head. "And he almost saved Greece from a bad king, but the Greeks turned on him, and they went with the king."

"Does he live in Greece?" Tommy Breen asks without a stutter.

"Poisoned himself. Swallowed the ink from his pen," Nicholas answers, almost whispering now.

Mary Wiles asks Miss D to make Nicholas K. change how his story ends. Nicholas K. is a liar, Mary says, and he has obviously made the whole story up, and so now he can change how it ends.

Mary is right about one thing: It is not the ending that we had hoped for—not for Tommy Breen, not for Nicholas K., not for any of us.

Miss D asks Nicholas K. if he wants to change his story, but he shakes his head *no* and says, "That's how it went: The Greeks gave up on Demosthenes, and Demosthenes gave up on them, and so he swallowed his ink."

We brace ourselves for the long contest with the fifth-grade boys and we steady ourselves in the absence of mercy. As if for consolation, Demosthenes is somehow down from his perch and propped up cheerfully on Nicholas K.'s desk. A faceless and digit-less figure carved from pine, no more than a foot in height, Demosthenes had always seemed an unlikely model for the human form.

Today, however, he seems to have a soul.

October, 1983

You would have been proud of me on August sixth! Ruthie and I, along with about ten Quakers of assorted ages and sex, stood in silent vigil on Main Street, Orleans, holding huge placards proclaiming our denunciation of nuclear warfare. Many who passed raised their thumbs in approbation, but others in another gesture. One man yelled, "Get off welfare, you slob!" I didn't deserve that epithet because I was wearing my best clothes, although you couldn't see them under the banner.

Yours,

D

Ex-Patriots

It is Glen Rooney's turn to lead us in the Pledge of Allegiance. With his right hand pressed to his chest, his short-sleeved cotton shirt hangs stiffly from his thin alabaster arm. He has lifted the visor to his astronaut's helmet as if to commune with us, but he has turned away from us and toward the flag, and we can hardly hear him. Miss D stands beside him and follows his lead. Like Glen, she pushes her own hunched shoulders back and stands with a new military posture; like Glen, she recites the Pledge in a staccato measure that keeps us all halting and trailing her in our own recitation.

I p-ledge a-LEE-gance

We have become so accustomed to Glen wearing his helmet that we run to his defense when other children mock him. We tell them to leave him alone, and that some day he'll be a famous astronaut, and that *dreamers are doers!* We say this last part the way Miss D always says it, with theatrical pace and punctuation, and we let the idea work on us. *Dreamers are doers.*

In a town where dreams are whiskey-induced, and where our parents piously wait for their numbers to come up in the lottery or through their bookies, Miss D offers us a new religion. "Don't look back!" she calls to us if we falter during a poetry recitation, or if we shake our heads *no* when she calls upon us. "Don't look back, darling!" She calls to us, "Jump! Jump!" It is scripture from the Church of Nonconformists. Don't look back for a reason to fail, she might have said to

57

us. Jump, before North Weymouth forbids it; before your parents forbid it; before your culture, your religion, or your worldview forbids it.

During science lesson one day, Miss D tells us—as if it is part of our study of the earth's atmosphere—that dreams are not airy things; that they are material things; that they come from the earth's elements, and that they come from what she calls *the here and now*. And, if dreams come from the here and now, Miss D tells us, then we should make our dreams out of the here and now.

It makes sense to us, therefore, that Glen Rooney—future astronaut—should wear an astronaut's helmet; that Nicholas Kastinopoulos, future ambassador to Greece, should proudly sport his Greek attire; and that for those among us with talents in painting or in writing, and whose names are listed on the blackboard under "Who's Who in Art"—there is always an ample supply of paint, paper, and pencils.

This morning, Glen Rooney is all persona, and Miss D makes it plain to us that she and the rest of us will be his understudies. We pledge allegiance in short staccato strides because of Glen's lead, but also because the pledge is parsed out in phrases all around our classroom. Although we have been reciting the pledge every morning since we were six years old, we cannot resist following the words in print—parcels of a pledge, like stations of the cross, on poster boards lining our walls.

When John G. Ashe objects that we are ten years old, and we certainly know the Pledge of Allegiance and we do not need it plastered on our walls, a few of the girls hush the rest of us quiet, and we wait for the terrible justice that comes to a boy who challenges an adult. But Miss D only pauses to look at John G. Ashe's intense eyes. She nods her head slightly and tugs on the hem of her vest with one hand while she smooths her other palm over her hair. It is a gesture that we have seen many times, a gesture that she reserves for tipping our expectations. "Very good," she says to John G. Ashe. "Very good."

After recess, we notice that the poster boards with the Pledge of Allegiance are gone. Miss D asks us to consider what we should put on our walls instead, and she appoints John G. Ashe as *Marshal of Arts*. Within a week, he and a few of the other boys whom he has handpicked have peeled the walls of scotch tape and hung up their own drawings instead: pictures of ships and cubist-like boys throwing out lines of rope; pictures of boys jumping off the Fore River Bridge, headfirst into the waters below, their arms like broken wings. When it seems as though John G. Ashe and his friends have enjoyed this inaugural showing for long enough, others begin to tape their drawings to the wall as well. For the rest of the year, pictures and poems will cover our walls with a kind of seasonal cycle and a spirit of competition that, without any directives from Miss D, we alone orchestrate: a row of Easter baskets, a chain of Christmas trees, a short sequence of menorahs, a series of pumpkins. Sabrina Kaslov decides that she should judge these seasonal art shows, and so now and then a first-place ribbon with a coveted gold medallion will hang from one of the drawings.

For a long time, hanging below our American flag is a display of our whole-class project: *American Ex-Patriots*. It is a misspelling of the word that we would not discover until much later in our lessons at Johnson Elementary. For now, it is a label that Miss D has crafted for us in thick, italicized letters—an error on her part, or perhaps a happy and intentional blending of ancient word origins with our shipyard origins. "Patriot," Miss D announced as she pointed to the placard peeking out from below our flag, "from the Latin for *home*." And "*Ex*, meaning *gone from home*." We cannot imagine ourselves gone from home. Hemingway, Gertrude Stein,

Man Ray, and images of Paris, the City of Light, crowd into the bulletin board that peeks out from under the flag. Miss D loves expatriates and we are encouraged to love them too—not because they reject America, but because, as she says, "It takes a rebel to get things roused." The rebel rouses the believer to explain himself. The expatriate rouses the patriot to defend himself. They seem to need each other, the way Miss D explains it. After a while, the difference between patriots and ex-patriots seems blurred to us too, since, according to Miss D, they are companions of a sort. From Hemingway to Robert Louis Stevenson, from Gertrude Stein to Copernicus, from Man Ray to Odysseus, the lesson is always the same: *In life, we must leave our homelands so that we can truly know our homelands.* We become expatriates in order to feel our patriotism. In art, we become dissidents in order to say our native allegiances more beautifully.

When Nicholas Kastinopoulos objects that he will never leave North Weymouth because he will never leave his uncles and his mother, and he would be a quitter not to work in the Shipyard too, Miss D hears that.

"The ex-patriot never leaves home," Miss D says to Nicholas K. and to all of us, "because home is up here"—and she points to her head. Home, she will show us again and again, is the place where we do our best work, the place where we make our best art, the place where we think our clearest and boldest thoughts. In choosing Paris over Ohio, bullfights over rodeo, Hemingway chose his home, his subject—a subject that drew from him all that he had. And for Miss D, and ultimately for all of us, choosing one's subject seemed to be the single most heroic task ahead of us—much more heroic than memorizing allegiances.

In his own adaptation of this idea, Bailey Arnold will routinely pack up his pencil and paper and leave his desk to resume his work somewhere else—his favorite place, on the concrete floor in the hallway outside our classroom door.

Each time he shuffles past us, John G. Ashe will look up from his work and in an exasperated tone, he will ask Bailey Arnold, "Where do you think *you're* going?"

"Home," Bailey Arnold will smugly reply. Miss D and the rest of us will watch silently as Bailey Arnold sets himself down on the concrete floor in the cold and quiet hallway and pulls his knees up to his chest for a makeshift desk and begins to write.

Home is up here.

Miss D's words seem to echo in the hallway where Bailey Arnold has planted himself. *Home is where we do our best work, where we think our clearest thoughts.* And we cannot help but notice that, until now, we have never seen Bailey Arnold bow his head to his paper like this; we have never seen Bailey Arnold follow his pencil across his page like this.

Over time we come to understand Miss D's notions of being who we are because we *choose* to be that way; of living in a place because we *choose* to live there. Each time we recite our pledge, there is the sense that we are choosing our allegiances, directing our own lives. A vague ebullience overtakes us, something akin to the joy that must come in spotting a crack of light in a prison wall. We pity our peers, who have never felt this open choice, who have never been tourists in their own town; who, after wandering from their roots, have never come back home to feel the deep sense of home and country that we feel in Room 20.

Conversely, with each daily pledge, there is always the chance that one of us might resist—that one of us might not stand and recite the Pledge of Allegiance, that one of us might reject this pledge as easily as the rest of us embrace it. When a few of the boys stay in their seats, rather than rise to recite the pledge one morning, Miss D asks them later if they are going somewhere.

"Leaving port, boys? Found a new home?" Miss D asks them.

When the boys laugh and tell her that they just didn't feel like reciting, a few of the girls gasp and Miss D looks at the boys as if they are speaking a foreign language. This is an idleness, a kind of dull inertia that she—and by now, the rest of us—detests.

"Up or down, boys! Sword or crown!" she shouts above our heads as she paces back and forth in front of us, "but, know our reasons why!"

It is a verse from a poem that we had written collectively during our study of the French Revolution; a poem about kings and freedom fighters, about fighting or not fighting. It was a poem about choices.

Sword or crown

Ground or Sky

But know our reasons why

Always this year, there has been the choice between sword or crown; always, this very new idea that we can participate—or not; that we can someday leave this town—or stay; that we can reject our inherited sea ports—or defend them. Always, since we entered Room 20, there has been the choice between two ways of living, where there had previously been no choice at all. And, always, there has been the implication from Miss D that, no matter which course we choose, it will be open and navigable to us—as long as we can explain ourselves:

Sword or crown, ground or sky, but know our reasons why.

November, 1983

And so I encourage you to not worry too much about what the future holds, darling. Every new place is a place of manifestation. Move toward that place and see from there who you are!

Lovingly,

Miss D

Moving Day

Quickly, darlings!" Miss D is shouting to us from the base of a waterfall—a cascade of pencils crashing to the floor, of geography texts thundering to their pathetic deaths of split open spines, and sheets of loose-leaf taking to the air like stinging white spray.

"Find your colleagues!"

It is the first Monday of the new month. Moving Day. This is the day, since our second month with Miss D, when we leave our old desks to take up residence at a new desk in a new row. It is a career move.

Often, amid the chaos, we see a brilliant choreography of ten-year-old girls joining arms and winging their way toward their new lives. It is a choreography that results from a previous weekend of intense planning—phoning friends and lobbying neighborhood playmates to choose a career that will place them in the same row of desks. For a month, we will live together in our distinct rows as singers, or senators, or painters, or bankers, or veterinarians, or poets, or nurses, or pilots, or engineers.

Some take this move more seriously than others: rags and scrub pads brought from their homes; buckets of water and soap stolen from the custodian's closet. There is a feeling in the air of the year starting over, a sense of ritual renewal that comforts us, but that also confuses us. Thus the red-haired boy whom we have come to know as the "D" student looks oddly ebullient and resourceful today, happy to shed his old skin; on the other hand, the silky-haired "A" student stands awkwardly by her old desk as if to guard the memory of an earned respect.

For others, moving will always mean *moving away*. In the next-to-last seat in the last row, the girl-with-the-bruises is lost in a labyrinth of circles and circles of soapsuds on her desktop. She finger-paints shapes that, on gray afternoons, in just the right light, will resurface like ghosts undiminished and whole: a six-petal rose and a beautiful cruciform quadrant.

"An artist," Miss D once told us, "turns grief into beautiful things." And in one swift blur, Miss D brandished a blade and cut off her own ear. We passed her ear around that day, while Miss D dotted stars onto an easel. The ear was made of a joke-shop fleshy rubber, but this was no joke. For the rest of the year, we would find ourselves talking to Miss D's "good ear" whenever we approached her with questions. She would turn the other ear toward us, as if to reassure us—but it was too late. The shift had already occurred: never again would we allow the facts to veil more pressing truths.

This afternoon's light cuts a sharp divide through the room. A few of us pause to revere the girl-with-the-bruises—*an artist*. The rest of us continue to gather our belongings and change places, and we scrub and scrub until our desks reflect our quiet and changing faces.

Cup Cake Hill, Tic Tock Terrace, Wall Street, Hollywood Boulevard. Though the residents change, the names of the rows never do. It is after the morning's lessons and after lunch. Miss D tells us that we have had enough time to *lose our bearings*. She is gliding up and down the rows, shaking our hands and saying, "Hello" and "How nice to meet you."

This is good theater—her greeting us as if we have never met—so we play along. Even now, though, the notion of a self-fashioned life is not lost on us. Beyond the Shipyard's morning toll, beyond our parents' lives of time cards and a bookie's promise, beyond the silky rings of whiskey by our cereal bowls, Miss D is pointing to other options. She is meeting our new selves—and in an unexpected way, we are meeting her anew too. Katherine Arthur Dunning, the woman from New Rochelle College—the woman who our parents say is *raising Cain*—has skin like Ivory soap, breath like chocolate mist, shoulders permanently hunched to a fourth-grader's height, and eyes as blue as ice on a mountain lake. Eyes wide open, she waits for something remarkable from us. We hate to let her down:

"And whom, may I ask, are *you*?" she asks.

"A navy pilot."

"An ace!" Miss D exults.

"A nurse."

"Florence Nightingale!"

"A painter."

"Our own Van Gogh!"

We say it in two parts—ours and hers. An exercise in prayer, in dreaming in pairs. This is heresy, but we cannot resist its appeal. Beyond our mothers' lives of scentless gin and scheduled days, there are these other lives, these choices. While our fathers play their numbers against the odds, we are banking on our own ingenuity. Miss D shakes us out of our caste system of delivered lives and requires instead self-made lives. We take from her lessons the material that we will need for our own metamorphoses. Surgeons, not students, we graft this material onto our skin, try it on for size, imagine new selves. While our parents wait for their ships to come in, we build ports for our leaving. And as if we know that this sort of self-fashioning is not part of the fourth-grade curriculum, we keep our plans to ourselves.

❧

At the end of Hollywood Boulevard is a cul-de-sac named

Speaker's Corner, where shelves overflow with poems, and sheet music, and troubled lives: Robert Louis Stevenson and his difficult wife; Rupert Brook's broken heart; Sandburg's fragile dreams for a democracy; Edwin Arlington Robinson's drunken songs; Dickinson's muffled cries; Whitman's howl. It is an Everyman's land, a place where we all go at one time or another, alone, disarmed; the place that Miss D also calls *The Well*. We go there for poems—poems that we'll say again and again, until we are ready to recite them the following Friday; poems beyond our years and that we say in our beds before drifting off:

> *Instead of lovers, love will be!*

or

> *Well this side of Paradise,*
> *There's little comfort in the wise!*

Or on the walk home from school:

> *Two roads diverged in a wood, and I –*
> *I took the one less traveled by,*
> *And that has made all the difference*

Or jumping rope:

> *Keeping time, time, time*
> *In a sort of Runic rhyme*
> *In the tintinnabulation that so musically wells*
> *From the bells, bells, bells, bells*
> *Bells, bells, bells*

Or playing tag:

> *We sailed along for days and days,*
> *And had the very best of plays;*
> *But Tom fell out and hurt his knee*
> Tag!
> *So there was no one left but me!*
> You're it!

In fact, we go to Speaker's Corner for rhythms more than poems—rhythms that we can move to, and after a while, rhythms that seem to adjust our step, our pulse, as well.

Today, however, we hear not a pulse, but an incredible roar. John G. Ashe, who has taken his place among the engineers, is refusing to take part in the Moving Day greetings. "You know who I am!" He is shouting at Miss D and he is pushing his desk away, as if to leave without leaving. We have all taken part in the game, so his outburst is now against us as well. We feel ourselves teetering on the tremor in John's raw voice. Miss D is smoothing her hair, and then her starched slacks, as if to clear two spaces—ours and John's. "You know who I am," John G. Ashe is shouting at her, "so don't act like you don't!"

"Darling," Miss D says, as she leans into the very edge of her newfound bubble. "I don't know who you are." And now she is swaying toward us, to let us in, to make this our answer too. "Every day, we are growing. And today—today I don't even know who I am!"

It is this last part that rattles us. How could our teacher not know who she is? We feel the introductions take a turn for the worse, or for the better—we are not sure which. Miss D seems to feel the turn too. She leans on a desk abandoned in all of the moving, and she smooths her hair until it seems to shine.

John G. Ashe is whispering that she is crazy, that everyone knows it, that his father is going to have her fired—and that he hates her—*hates* her.

December, 1983

When people criticize me, I know they are speaking the Gospel truth.

Ever yours,

D

A MIDDLE PATH

Recess when we should be doing long division. But we finished math long ago, almost in the same instant that we started it. Above us, through frosted windows, we feel the jealous stares of peers pretending to be sharpening pencils, of teachers resigned to the temperate indoors. But for us it is more than an escape from lessons; it is the triumph of our own tracks in fresh snow; to feel the flakes like paper ice crunching beneath our feet. The season's first flurries.

For Miss D, it is a kind of body prayer, a middle path that we make across our playground, a trail we make without trying. To feel—and then forget—the wet cold settling in our shoes, then in our socks, then in the sagging hems of the starched print dresses that the pretty girls wear. To let the elements take hold, to welcome chance.

Somehow, we need this walk. At times, she leads; at other times, she drifts off to the left or to the right, to watch us move in *S* shapes and in circles. With no one to guide us, we cut a path together, across the film of white and patchy-green that was our playground, but that now—without a proper recess bringing us here—is nowhere at all.

Miss D claps and smiles and teeters as we pass, and we clap back—our hands too frozen to perform the usual sounds, our mouths too stiff to make proper smiles. In cold like this, one has to make adjustments.

We march without a worry. All is forgiven.

February, 1984

Two a.m. and reading R.L.S. again. I've always loved his deep compassion for the fallen angel.

Yours,

D

FALLEN ANGELS

In a tone that she usually reserves for announcements of no real consequence, Miss D informs us one rainy morning that the Bad Behavior Book is now the Big Ideas Book. It is a revolutionary move. According to John G. Ashe's complaint, it is downright tyranny.

A massive tome of empty pages that apparently comes with the classrooms at Johnson Elementary School and that occupies the corner of a teacher's desk, the Bad Behavior Book is where the bad child—the soon-to-be-penitent one, the one who needs our prayers and the prayers of all the saints—will scribble his own cursed name as proof of his mutiny at Johnson Elementary School. It is a lawyer's evidence for parents on *Meet Your Teacher Night*: names of the lost souls in our class. It is our Book of the Dead.

In changing its name from the Bad Behavior Book to the Big Ideas Book, Miss D announces to us that there are some labels that she does not want recorded in ink. Tucked behind our desks, we watch her as she feverishly crosses out the names of the guilty until, apparently unhappy with their shadowy permanence, she tears the pages from the book. It is our first attendance at an exorcism.

For the majority of us—even the bad children—these are labels that we will not give up easily. Handing over these classifications will require our starting again, establishing new identities, imagining new criteria for who will be loved and who will be disinherited, who will be remembered warmly and who will be condemned. These were identities that we had worked hard to acquire—personal profiles, like overtures that precede us as we move from grade to grade at Johnson Elementary. This, John G. Ashe objected, would be meddling at a whole new level.

As if unclear about the revolutionary change that Miss D has put into place—or perhaps resistant to her brand of forgiveness and renewal—the bad children continue to fill this massive book with their names. At first, when Miss D calls their names out from the book and asks them to stand and share with us their big ideas, they stand, heads hung, shoulders rounded, characteristically ashamed.

"Chin up," Miss D calls out. "We want to hear your big idea!"

And when the one who has been called upon claims to have forgotten his or her big idea, Miss D calls on the rest of us to put our heads together. "We will help. We will come up with a big idea."

It is only a few weeks before several of us have lined up to inscribe our own names into the Big Ideas Book. We know that we could be called upon now, and that we must be ready to surprise Miss D and the others with something that they never could have imagined—something shocking, or brilliant, or hilarious, or daring.

More often than not, when Miss D does call on us, we stutter an inarticulate but no-less big idea—but we know, somehow, that this is not our real work. We have sensed a shift in paradigm. Although we cannot know its implications, we see that by playing along with Miss D we have participated in something bigger: We have given the bad child a second chance; we have given him back his good name. We have allowed him to save face, to go on living, to consider metamorphosis. At least for the time being, we have changed our label for him from bad child to simply *child*—and in doing so, we have somehow changed ourselves as well.

March, 1984

Spend all you have for loveliness,
Buy it and never count the cost;
For one white singing hour of peace
Count many a year of strife well lost
And for a breath of ecstasy
Give all you have been or could be.

Sara Teasdale, darling, talking to both of us this time.
Sending love,

D

VIRTUOSO

As seasoned fourth-graders, we have learned that the branding of some children as *bad* or *slow* does have one advantage: It prizes the unbranded. In spite of a new fellowship that we are beginning to feel among us in Room 20, we cannot help but wonder if perhaps the principal and the other teachers were right after all. Perhaps we should fight for our hard-earned identities as A students and D students; perhaps we should protect these hard-earned labels. Perhaps John G. Ashe was right. Perhaps we should stay in our teacher-assigned rows. For all of our unspoken deliberation, neither the unbranded nor the branded can get through to Miss D.

The more that Bailey Arnold tries to reveal himself to Miss D as one of the branded, the more Miss D seems to see him as saved. After one of his best performances of forced burping at every pause during the Pledge of Allegiance one morning, Miss D names Bailey Arnold not an agitator, not a hellion, not a rascal. These would have been labels he had heard before and understood. Instead, Miss D names Bailey Arnold a *virtuoso*.

"Bailey Arnold," Miss D soberly calls out to him, "you do have a musical ear."

In disbelief, the rest of us drop our palms from our hearts, but we remain standing. We are waiting for Miss D to deliver to Bailey Arnold his sentence for his crime. Those of us who have come up through the grades with Bailey Arnold remember that forced burping during the Pledge of Allegiance was a serious infraction in the second grade. By the third grade, it was high treason, and cause to move Bailey Arnold's desk into the storage closet of the classroom, his narrow and traitorous back facing us for the rest of the year.

By the fourth grade, we have absorbed these laws that our teachers have taught us as the only true principles; balances of justice like noble ratios—ratios of crime to expectation, of misdeed to school rule, of punishment to the changed heart. Miss D seems woefully unaware of these delicate balances. Eventually, we will recognize that she simply rejects them. In fact, by the end of the year, we will come to reform our notions of social justice as well. When the principal announces that we will need a Grand Marshall to lead the sixth-graders in their graduation procession, Bailey Arnold will be the obvious choice—not just for Miss D, but for all of us. For months, since that day when he was anointed as Maestro of Music, Bailey Arnold has led us through Thanksgiving hymns, Christmas carols, and even in our transitions from one lesson to another. Two claps of his small, pale hands, and we shuffle through our desks for our workbooks; two more claps—or perhaps his extraordinary pretend burp—and we are quietly waiting for Miss D to start our lesson.

To the majority of us, it is all a ridiculous joke, and yet after a while we come to rely upon this tempo that Bailey Arnold sets for us. When Bailey Arnold is sick at home for a week, Nicholas K. tries to take his place—stomping his foot twice for us to fall into line for recess, or starting our quiet reading time with an inaugural farting noise that he makes with his hand in his armpit. But it is not the same, and so we tell Nicholas K. that he is not Bailey Arnold—not even close—and a few of the motherly girls make Get Well cards for Bailey Arnold.

Still we worry for our own good health. Those of us, who have paid attention in grades one through three have seen that there is always a tipping point when it came to boys like

Bailey Arnold. The harder we try to lure Miss D back into a system that we know will work for us, the more she seems to return its broken parts to us. In the same week that she and the majority of us appoint Bailey Arnold as Music Maestro, Timothy Martin and some of the mean boys exercise their most ambitious pranks. Oddly, Miss D seems to see their pranks not as punishable, not as praiseworthy—but as fertile ground somehow.

When Timothy Martin falls out of Miss D's coat closet as she reaches inside, Miss D does not faint from fear; she does not send Timothy Martin by the seat of his pants to the powers that be. Instead she stomps her foot hard and hollers, "Tres bien! O that took forethought," she gasps almost appreciatively, and "How did you stay so quiet?"

She seems to not understand that this is cause for a trip to the principal's office.

Instead, as if Timothy Martin's prank has promoted him to position of Teacher's Aide, Miss D asks him if he would please put his *Steady-Teddiness* to more use—and could he help her hang up a new poster? From our seats, we watch Timothy Martin tremble and teeter on the top of a ladder while he tacks up Miss D's new banner. A series of pages that unfolds like an accordion, the banner features cartoon-like drawings of faces that we ultimately recognize as our own—self-portraits that we drew in our first few weeks in Room 20.

We tilt our heads back and we see Sabrina Kaslov's almond-shaped eyes and her long auburn hair tied back in a red velvet ribbon that she has glued on for a mesmerizing, mixed media effect. We see Nicholas K.'s square chin, his Hellenic nose, and his deep sienna eyes. We see Glen Rooney's astronaut's helmet wrapped snugly around his head, his aquamarine eyes peering out at us as if from a distant planet. Across the top of the banner in oily black cursive letters, reads the title:

ALL PRESENT!

Long after Timothy Martin is secure in his seat, Miss D remains looking up at the banner that he has hung for her. With her back to us, she points to the banner and reads it to us as if we might otherwise miss its message:

"ALL PRESENT!"

She parses out the words the way our first-grade teacher parsed out the pages of our *Dick and Jane* books. Except for the shuffling of the feet of a few of the boys, the majority of us sit numbly behind our desks wondering what we are missing. This is code; this much we know. Miss D helps us. Turning herself away from the banner and toward us, she seems to crack the code for us.

"All present!" she repeats, and then leaning toward us as if to conspire with us, or as if counting on us to shock her with our brilliance, she asks us in a whisper,

"Now what?"

We tip our heads back again to study our own faces: delicately penciled outlines in a palette of familiar skin tones: tan, sienna, alabaster, and bronze. Nothing more than a likeness to our current selves. For the first time at Johnson Elementary, we recognize Miss D's question as entirely ours to answer.

PART II

Spring

April, 1984

Teaching is so filled with doubts. I often thought that ditch digging would be easier. I never thought I was very good, and ended so many days despairingly. As for your last letter, I felt privileged to be included in your own professional doubts. But, you know, my dear pupil, that you are more intelligent than I. My only gift is feeling and awareness.

Lovingly,

D

BUSY PEOPLE

It is Meet Your Teacher Night. Miss D seems to have forgotten to return our desks into this evening's expected rows, and so our parents move uncomfortably around the day's fading circles of chairs and desks. Preoccupied by their collective effort to find a space that is familiar, our parents edge their way past our Big Ideas Book, past Demosthenes, past our banner of self-portraits, and past our open notebooks on our desks with our *Welcome Parents* letters—letters like open hands left awkwardly extended.

Eventually, they take up their positions near a comforting clothesline of drying watercolors. Those of us who have come with our parents settle into our seats as if to enjoy a late-night convening of Congress. Miss D makes her way from parent to parent introducing herself and struggling to straighten her back to the height of adults.

Who is this woman who is half-standing, half-bowing before our parents? When the stock market crashed in October 1929, she was a young woman from a suburb of Boston finding her way through her first semester in college. A Catholic academy for women, New Rochelle College offered Caddy Dunning her Arcadia. The golden age of the 20s and 30s—with its innovations in radio, automobiles, aviation, and the telephone—had not entirely disappeared in the dusk of the Depression. When she graduated in 1932, she was what historians would later call an emblem of the Golden Age of Spinsters: single, self-supporting, a social activist, a smoker, and an educator.

In an era of *Misses* in public schools, she was a *fire starter.* *Education is not the filling of a pail, but the lighting of a fire,* the poet Yeats wrote. And, in what would seem a conscious invoking of his muses, Miss D would routinely begin our lessons each morning by leaning into our bourgeois block of desks-in-rows and whispering, "Let's light a fire." Not teacher, but incendiary. Not students, but firebrands. A provocateur, a rabble-rouser, whose preference for enlightenment in exchange for bell curves was drawing us in. Against North Weymouth's backdrop of generations of men making ships rise up like cathedrals; amid this town's seasonal mist of steel dust, salt air, and blended whiskey, Miss D struck a contrast: a modern woman, a cultured woman, an urban woman, a worldly woman.

However, from the looks on our parents' faces on Meet Your Teacher Night, as they hug the perimeter of Room 20, they see a different woman. Although Miss D is greeting each of our parents as though they are her long-lost friends, the majority of our parents offer stiff and oddly formal greetings in return. By contrast, Miss D cups our parents' hands when she shakes them:

"Oh, how wonderful that you came!"

Now and then Miss D stops in front of one of our parents so that she can guess which child the parent belongs to.

"Oh, you must be John G. Ashe's father! Yes? Yes! I know those noble ears!"

In her apparent excitement, Miss D continues to hold tight onto one mother's hand even after she has begun to lead the rest of the parents around our classroom to show them our art and our big ideas. It is a surprisingly long and difficult tour. Our parents appear to be as uncomfortable bending to the height of Miss D's bowed shoulders—her bowed perspective—as she seems physically pained by her effort to straighten to meet them.

❧

Apparently the biggest surprise of all on Meet Your Teacher Night is Mrs. Arnold's disbelief that her son, Bailey Arnold, has not been commissioned to the corner of the classroom. For those of us who have come up from the third grade with Bailey Arnold, this is our constant wonder as well. Although he and his desk will resume their customary place in the corner of the classroom in the fifth grade, for the here and now he is one of a very elite group. He is one of what Miss D calls *The Busy People*.

The Busy People sit in the first seat of every row because they have myriad responsibilities. They turn lights off and then on again during slide shows; they open windows and close them; they collect math problems and return them; they collect milk money and distribute milk cartons; they sharpen pencils—some more expertly than others. They marshal us down the slick and polished stairwell for fire drills; they erase the board; they let out a visceral *Sssshhhhhhh* when Miss D wants our attention. We are under strict orders from Miss D not to bother The Busy People when they are doing their schoolwork, because—as Miss D tells us—we can only imagine the burden of responsibilities that they have outside of our usual tasks.

To many of us The Busy People are turncoats—discipline problems turned deans. To Miss D, however, they are celestial—paragons of energy and promise; our champions somehow. And yet, including them in our long-established hierarchy means throwing off much of what we have learned up until now: making sense of our own lives by labeling others; edging some of us out so that some can stay in; making tall better than small; fair-haired better than dark; porcelain skin better than freckled; smart better than slow. Strong. Pretty. Bright. Quiet. Obedient. These were all of the *better-thans* that we had paid attention to during our last three years and that we had so diligently mastered.

When John G. Ashe complained to Miss D that she was

turning everything upside down by letting *bad* kids do *good-kid* chores, she took more time than usual in answering him. She moved to the middle of the classroom and said in a whisper, "Would the *bad* children please raise their hands?"

Bailey Arnold started to lift his arm, but the girl behind him hissed at him and swatted it down. Miss D looked all around the classroom, stretching her neck as though trying to imitate the most earnest of searchlights. And then: "Would the *good* children please raise their hands?"

John G. Ashe raised his hand, then Sabrina Kaslov, and then a few of the pretty girls. The classroom erupted. Mary Wiles objected that John G. Ashe had no business raising his hand, since he took the last ice cream at lunch and he is the most selfish boy that she ever knew. Some of the motherly girls got on their feet: one closing the door to the school hallway, others conferring with one another. When Nicholas Kastinopoulos turned the lights on and off—a technique for getting our attention that he learned from our third grade teacher—and told us that he had an announcement to make, we listened to him because he was bigger than most of us, more man than boy, and because he insisted upon our listening.

"No more good and bad kid forever," Nicholas K. sternly announced, "You're gonna have to earn it."

"Every day?!" John G. Ashe objected.

"Every day."

Nicholas K. bowed his head and returned to his seat as if to say *meeting adjourned*. We waited for Miss D's intervention, but she was neatly tucked behind her desk and out of range. She had been watching us; her only contribution: folded hands, a smile, and a raised eyebrow.

Sabrina Kaslov shrugged her shoulders, slipped her No. 2 pencil out of its velvet sleeve and returned to the math problem on her desk. The rest of us followed suit. The cool, clear water of arithmetic for the time being. After a while the only sound that we heard was the scratching of pencils and Miss D's drone humming—and her periodic gasps of wonder—as she poured over our morning compositions.

୧

The day after Meet Your Teacher Night, Bailey Arnold will call for a celebration for the best Meet Your Teacher Night ever. But, phantom doubts dog us. While in line for recess, some of us will innocently replay our parents' comments from the night before.

"What good is a clock that doesn't work?" John G. Ashe suddenly asks Miss D after weeks of not asking.

"Shouldn't we have announcements on our Daily Announcements board?" Nicholas K. bleats out.

"I'll bet the fifth-graders' clock works," Sabrina Kaslov mutters.

None of us tells them to be quiet, not even the motherly girls whom we have come to regard by now as the guardians of good manners. As if Miss D discerns all at once our mutiny and our confusion—and perhaps even the apologies that we will want to say later—she bows to us one after the other as we exit the classroom for the playground.

"Good nobles," she says as she bends towards us, "go make your marks."

୧

While none of us will ever see a Pink Slip, we expect it any day now. Time and again, we have heard from our peers on the playground that Miss D is going to get the Pink Slip, and we wait for this event like understudies to an utterly, unplayable lead role. On one occasion, when the principal's secretary appears in our doorway with an early-dismissal slip for someone's doctor's appointment, our hearts stop. We know, each time that the secretary appears for various reasons, that the slip that she holds in her hand is Miss D's dismissal slip.

We dread the Pink Slip, not only because we fear losing

Miss D, but also because we are like apprentices who fear that, in her absence, we just might surrender. We might surrender to the sedative of a school calendar—rather than our own ticking hearts. We might concede to the orthodoxy of showing our steps in math problems—rather than showing our leaps of genius. We might buckle under the iterative rule of honoring all adults—rather than just those who live honorably. We might capitulate to the bell curve of realistic goals—rather than prove our potential.

We are not ready for Miss D to be gone. We cannot imagine her gone. And yet, as much as we want to, we cannot imagine her safely here.

May, 1984

For one child's sake
may childhood ever be
a land of wonder and
delight. May everyone
upon the earth be free
to live and learn and
set the wrong aright.

I loved this prayer so much that I thought I would share it with you. I am tired in my bones. Last Thursday, I spent hours in silent vigil at the entrance to Otis Air Field protesting the manufacturing of missile parts. I did it to support Ruth's convictions. My own needs for peace are less global, but just as hard to come by.

Ever yours,

D

POWER LUNCH

It is something akin to the convening of Congress. Miss D says that it is common for very powerful people to come up with very powerful ideas over lunch. So once a month we form a circle with our desks, while Miss D passes around a basket of fresh fruit and chocolates. Since our second week of school, the power lunch has been our way to discuss issues of the day—usually things about school that we would like to change, but sometimes we talk about things outside of school as well.

By now, we have created our own hierarchy of principal speakers. Miss D tells us the titles and appointments, but the assignments are our own and this is our Congress: Nicholas Kastinopoulos as Master of Ceremonies; John G. Ashe as Student Principal; and Sabrina Kaslov as Secretary, which gives her a chance to use her new feather quill pen that she got for her birthday.

Nicholas Kastinopoulos opens each lunch with a quote from a giant and tattered book that he borrows from Miss D's desk: *A History of Greek Ideas*. Each time, he reads us something from Socrates, or from the mature Achilles, or from the god-fearing Odysseus. We love the panache with which he delivers these openings and while the motherly girls giggle behind their cupped palms, the rest of us clap and hoot for him. Miss D loves Nicholas K.'s quotes so much that she often leaps to the board to transcribe them.

At every power lunch, John G. Ashe sits to the right of Nicholas K. due to one idea that he had. It was John G.

Ashe's idea that Johnson Elementary School should have a Student Principal—someone who works side-by-side with the principal, someone who makes sure that grades one through six are truly represented. We liked his idea so much that we elected him Principal Ex Officio, a title that Miss D recommended. Forever after, John G. Ashe would be the messenger who delivers things to the office for Miss D. Upon each return from the principal's office, he will tell us that he has had a word with the principal about this or that—and we will listen intently for a recap of our own ideas: "Isn't recess too short?" "Isn't the school year too long?" "Why not have art twice a week?" "Wouldn't a swimming pool be nice?" "And we could skate on it in the winter!"

Sometimes John G. Ashe attaches his own list of items to Miss D's messages when he delivers them for her. We know this because the principal comes to our classroom now and then for what he calls *an informal visit*. He walks up and down our aisles and does not speak to us. He touches Bailey Arnold's shoulder, which makes him pop up like a jack-in-the-box; he looks over our backs at the work we are doing; he points to errors on Mary Wiles's math worksheet, which sets her furiously erasing and starting again; and just before he leaves, he always returns John G. Ashe's list of items to him, saying, "Thank you, Mr. Ashe."

In order to keep a record of John G. Ashe's recycled ideas, Miss D suggests we post them on one of our classroom bulletin boards. Now and then, a few of us quietly add our own ideas to the board until, after a while, John G Ashe's crumpled notes are framed by a cacophony of wishes and dreams.

The writers of the *Declaration of Independence* would have loved this kind of drafting board, Miss D tells us. "It's a collage of our dreams and desires," she announces, arms crossed and clearly admiring it. A place to post our hopes, our yearnings, our complaints, our dreams—our visions of future places, future schools, future worlds. *Our prayer wall,* Miss D labels it on one occasion. If, decades later, educators would become practitioners of the theology of self-esteem, for now, Miss D would teach us self-government.

Some of us use this new opportunity for free expression to post grand and optimistic ideas. There are Sabrina Kaslov's *Thirteen Amendments to Recess Rules* tacked in shimmering metallic and royal blues. Others use this new bulletin board to reveal their hearts' fears and prayers. Edged up against Sabrina's ambitious *Amendments* is a more cryptic proposal: An anonymous illustration in pencil and ink of an angry tall person and a sad small person. When John G. Ashe objects that the board is for posting ideas and not for art, the classroom erupts. Others have already followed the anonymous artist's lead and begun their own drawings for posting, and John G. Ashe is not Marshall of *all* Arts, we tell him. Miss D suggests we discuss this at our next Power Lunch and when we do, the decision is made: The bulletin board will not allow art.

A group of us feels crushed—crushed by the elegance of our own democracy. Miss D tries to console us by telling us it is our first lesson in living in a Republic and that we should feel confident that *there is no stopping a good idea.* It is a proposition that—along with Miss D—we will put on trial. As it turns out, it is a brief trial.

When it is time for the art to come down, Sabrina Kaslov seems to feel—more than the rest of us—the suddenly vacant space on the bulletin board beside her *Amendments.* She appoints herself Director of Art and Words and she announces that if we can only post words on the board, then all art will go to her committee for changing into words. As if to prove her qualifications for this new position, she draws herself up close to the pencil and ink illustration hanging on its last thumbtack. In words, she announces, this picture would say, "Grownups should not shout at children." Glen Rooney raises his astronaut's helmet, adjusts his glasses, and draws in closer to the illustration. "Grown-ups should not hurt us," he says, revising Sabrina's translation with a kind of editorial authority.

After a while, the bulletin board becomes a drafting board of all kinds: John G. Ashe's recycled and crumpled notes share a space with Sabrina Kaslov's baroque and ambitious proposals; pictures that seem too private or even blasphemous in another setting are sent to Sabrina's and Glen's committee and changed into gold and saffron commentaries for all to see and read. Bold thoughts, idealistic ideas, pictures changed into words. The bulletin board becomes our open canvas, our wailing wall, Jefferson's open notebook—and for Miss D, the best place for the best news.

June, 1984

I often thought in Room 20, wouldn't it be nice if we could bring the outside in and the inside out more often?

T.Y.,

D

FIELDWORK

Weeks after our monthly Power Lunch and long after The Busy People have erased Miss D's favorite quotes from the blackboard, we discover the same quotes written in beautiful Palmer script and taped to a wall in our classroom. They are so haphazardly stuck there that it is difficult to imagine even Miss D posting them up. It is as if they have blown into our classroom from the distant, dank past of ancient Greece and magically adhered to our windows and walls.

To the right of our classroom door, on a sharp right angle, such that we have to cock our heads to read it, in brilliant gold paint on a black poster backing, is the shimmering adage:

TO THINE OWN SELF BE TRUE

Or, suddenly taped to the door of the art closet, we find the sobering advice:

KNOW THYSELF

And, just above the blackboard, Achilles' shield reproduced in gold and saffron and silver, like a shield for each of us. These axioms and icons become our private discoveries, our personal prescriptions ready for our discovering at precisely the right moments in our lives. We happen upon them the way one might fall upon a code that no one else can unlock. Even as fourth-graders, we see them as Miss D's way of turning the lesson over to us, of lifting the lesson out of its original place and granting it new range—our range.

After a while, our classwork becomes our fieldwork. When a fifth-grader shoves Sabrina Kaslov on the playground one

Friday afternoon, she rises to her feet, brushes off her navy suit-dress with its pilgrim collar of stars and stripes, and bringing the tip of her nose to his, she warns him,

"Push me and you push the gods."

The rest of us know to step away. Sabrina Kaslov has always clearly been a favorite of the gods. Beautiful. Smart. Proud. Perhaps immortal. Throughout the year, she has drawn pictures of the Greek gods on her paper-bag book covers until they crowd the edges. When Nicholas Kastinopoulos once suggested that her Zeus should have a full, gray beard—and not the handsome square jaw that she had given him—she railed against him,

"How would *you* know?!"

And, when Nicholas K. did not answer, perhaps it was because he was wondering the same thing as the rest of us:

How does Sabrina Kaslov know?

It was as if Nicholas K. had offended her grandfather. He had certainly hurt some kinship that she had made with her subject. And, among the lessons we were learning this year, we had learned very early to honor kinships between heart and mind.

But it was on a school day a few weeks later when Sabrina's ire would be cause for our mobilizing our classroom lessons into something more palpable: by the time Tommy Breen tells Sabrina Kaslov that the fifth-grade boy on the playground was only playing and that he didn't mean to *sh-sh-sh-shove* her and that she doesn't have to have a *ffff-it* about it, the pretty girls have already surrounded Sabrina like a hierarchy of angels. Since the day we walked onto the playground at Johnson Elementary School, the fifth-grade boys have done almost nothing without meaning it. When the recess bell summons us back inside, we find ourselves answering to our own schedules—to our own balances of justice. Until now, we have understood our education at Johnson Elementary as separate from our true lives, a separation of school and dreams as sacred in North Weymouth as the separation of church and state.

But by now we are clearly carrying our lessons from Room 20 onto the field. *To thine own self be true. Know thyself. What would Socrates say? What would Gandhi do? What would Achilles want us to do?* When Nicholas K. draws Sabrina into our fold, the rest of us draw in too. We look out at the open range of our playground and we are determined to make it up to Sabrina and to her gods. We look up at the red brick walls of our school, heavy and apathetic under the gray winter sky. We wish it were as easy as joining our peers in their orderly line—and we wish it were as simple as lessons learned inside.

July, 1984

Your awareness and empathy will bring you more heartaches than most, but oh, darling, you will experience compensatory ecstasy! Our gifts and passions guide us. I've never known a fool with a working heart.

With so much love,

D

RIDDLING

April 1, 1967. A day of surprises and pranks for our peers, but for those of us in Room 20 at Johnson Elementary School it is the beginning of a new year. According to legend, and according to Miss D, the fools were the ones who resisted the changing of the New Year from April 1 to January 1. What should have been a quiet shift in empires—from the Julian to the Gregorian calendar—for the fools was a colonization: an exchange of spring for winter that they could not bear. And so the empire did what it had to do: It mocked the resisters and called them fools. Today, in Miss D's class we are all fools, foolishly and happily adhering to a Julian calendar. For a single day—at least in our class—there will be no division over calendars; no clash between Caesars; no drawing lines in the sand.

Celebrating the start of a new year on April 1st. This is all good fun, and yet, even now its value is not lost on us. For the first time in our lives, we feel the fluid and even arbitrary nature of how we mark time—calendars and holidays that emerge, not according to some absolute plan as we had previously thought, but according to the monarchy in place. While this revelation might set us off balance, instead we revel in it. We revel in this because, for the first time in all of our school years, we—"the fools"—are the monarchy in place. We not only hear about the creation of calendars, we choose one over the other. And for a single day we feel the power—but also the self-consciousness—that kings must feel.

Instead of April Fool's Day pranks that pit us against one another, there will be riddles and puzzles that draw us into a huddle for their figuring out. It is the part of the festivities that Miss D likes the best, especially the round-robin riddles. At any moment, she will point to one of us, and from there down the row, each of us will create a line for a riddle that the rest of the class will have to solve.

I come with thunder

And we all look to the next child in the row to add his or her line.

And I come with a storm
My fire can warm you
But usually I'll burn you!

All of us are quiet as we reflect on the lines we heard. Sabrina Kaslov has scribbled them down and a few of the pretty girls have gathered around her desk to hear her recite the lines again. Miss D bends over and leans both palms on her thighs, her head studying the floor. "I come with thunder?" she raises her head to ask.

"Yes!" one of the riddle-makers answers.

"And my fire can burn you!" someone shouts, helpfully.

Miss D never speaks beyond this first prompt, and she never offers answers, so we know it is up to us now. She keeps her head down, mumbling parts of the riddle to herself—"can warm, but usually it burns you"—while the rest of us work collectively. We forget Miss D is here and we shout out answers and questions at random among ourselves.

"Comes with a storm?"

"Yup!"

"Comes with thunder?"

"Yup!"

"Is it lightening?"

"No!"

"Is it the art teacher?"

[Laughter]

"No!"

"The principal!!"

A collective gasp wisps through the classroom. Without waiting for confirmation that the riddle has been solved, Sabrina Kaslov disbands her circle of pretties and soberly returns her No. 2 pencil to its velvet sleeve. A hush sweeps over the classroom, then muffled laughter.

Inevitably, the best riddles are the truth-telling ones; and each time we land on one, Miss D seems to react the same way. Even after so many months with her, we still expect to be scolded for our irreverence, but instead Miss D looks up at us with a glint in her eyes. A slow smile comes over her face, and then a raspy, volcanic laugh. She covers her mouth and bends over again, laughing. Our laughter and our voices cause a clatter throughout the classroom, and one of the motherly girls gets up to close our classroom door tight.

We will be a monarchy of truth-tellers. Riddles that surprise us with their candor; riddles that hush us and make us close our door tight—these are the best ones. We have learned by now about the aching truth in metaphor and many of us have become masters at it. Without question, the riddle-makers in the classroom hold a higher position than the rest of us—a kind of Brahmin-like status that Miss D endorses and that we all agree they deserve. There is nothing more dazzling and worthy of our admiration than a good riddle. A good riddle washes over us like a communal bath; it draws us into a circle to say what we know. It says what we are afraid to say, and it says it artfully. A good riddle reminds us that our fears need not make us mute and dumb—but, in fact, our fears might make us vocal and clever and sharp.

"It takes great fear to know how strong we are!" Miss D likes to say to us. And with every good riddle, we feel ourselves growing stronger.

Your daddy loves me
Morning, noon, and night

I go with eggs or steak or tea
I make his days seem bright
"Whiskey!"
"Too easy," someone objects.

The easy riddles make us impatient, and we demand harder ones. Even though extra points will go to riddles that rhyme, we push the riddle-makers to work harder, to rummage around in our thoughts and fears, to surprise us with their genius. To talk to us in code about the things we knew best:

The numbing effect of whiskey
The government of the strap
The relentless call of a shipyard's horn
The ever-present fear of layoffs
A reverence for routine
An aversion to the unexpected
The dull look in a principal's eye
The difference between hope and religion
The crippling call to conformity
The loneliness of being ten years old

These were things that we knew about in the fourth grade. But, until now, we had never imagined these as elements to examine or critique—or change. Certainly, until now, we had never imagined these as mobilizing, even catalytic elements.

But the riddlers were our mobilizers, our catalysts. Even for something as steeped in tradition as April Fool's Day with all of its requirements for pulling pranks and affirming hierarchies—students vs. teachers; beautiful girls vs. homely girls; strong boys vs. delicate boys—even these, we approached differently. For all of the quirky differences among us, we had become one, a collective, and we could not imagine hurting one another—not even for a laugh.

August, 1984

So often it's a tradeoff, darling—one thing for another. And I guess it doesn't take a genius in math to see the difference between a whole life lived or a fraction of a life lived.

All my love,

Miss D

FRACTIONS

When Miss D introduces us to the concept of fractions, it is a lesson in the human condition. Without looking our way, and without a word about opening our arithmetic books, she draws herself in close to the blackboard and sketches a headless figure in chalk. Still facing the blackboard and without turning toward us—apparently so as not to lose her focus—she turns her head to her side and addresses us over her shoulder:

"Children," she calls to us. "How should I draw a hero?"

This was going to take time. By the time the bell rings for the second lunch shift of fourth-graders and fifth-graders to file out into the playground, we are dug in. A hero would need a head, we all agree, and—according to Sabrina Kaslov—a large and loving heart. Glen Rooney insists on a soul, which he draws on the board as the Star of David, two perfectly intertwined triangles with long rays of chalk radiating out from them. As the afternoon sun cuts its way across our classroom, we ruminate aloud about the makeup of the perfect man. What part of the whole would be given to the head? The heart? The soul?

For John G. Ashe this is the most fundamental of all math problems: If the body has three parts, then each part will be one-third of the whole. His hero would be one-third head, one-third heart, and one-third soul. But for Glen Rooney, and for Nicholas Kastinopoulos, and for Sabrina Kaslov, and for many of us, this is clearly a riddle from a sphinx, or an oracle, or from the Old Testament's Samson himself.

"Aren't heroes special?" Glen Rooney asks in objection to John G. Ashe's simple math. "And so he can't be all normal in three equal parts!"

"If a man has more heart than head," Nicholas K. asks Miss D, "can he be a hero? Tommy Breen is clearly two-third's heart and one-third head and look how the fifth-graders pummel him all the time." And then, with his voice trailing off as if to reflect his own introspection, Nicholas K. asks Miss D and the rest of us, "And what about bully strength? Don't we need that to make a hero?" This added characteristic would clearly carve our hero into quarters rather than thirds; nevertheless, Miss D puts her hand to her chin and we all consider that. But before we can determine the degree to which a hero should be a physical animal, Sabrina Kaslov has moved on to the metaphysical.

"What exactly is a soul?" Sabrina Kaslov wants to know. "Isn't it the same as a heart?" Sabrina is at the blackboard pointing to Glen's illustration. But Glen Rooney's soul that he drew here looks just like a star. And he's the smartest boy in the class. "So stars and souls are the same," Sabrina neatly concludes, "That settles it!"

And yet we have never felt so unsettled. Open lunch bags on our desks, we are deep in the middle of something more akin to Aristotelian ethics rather than a lesson in fractions. While the math seems straightforward enough, it will be these other questions that will continue to haunt us. For several weeks afterward, as we raise our voices in protest against the principal's morning announcement of "Students Who Will Serve Detention"; as we reject his naming of names, we consider that figure on the board again. *What fraction of our time at Johnson Public Elementary School will be given to our souls? What fraction to our minds?* For Miss D, these appear to be easy math problems, but not so for the rest of us. Again and again, there are questions to consider—questions that Miss

D brings to us so deliberately that we are sure they will show up in our state-mandated test at the end of the year. But they never do.

It is always outside Room 20 that we find ourselves applying our lessons in arithmetic or history or literature. When the slightest, palest boy in our class triggers the terror of a sixth-grade teacher, Miss D's lesson in fractions is on our minds. For several weeks, while the fourth, fifth, and sixth-graders have marched single file down the custodian's slick and sparkling hallway to our morning recess—left hands by our sides, right forefingers held up tight against our closed lips as if to mime a communal hush—Teddy White has preferred not to walk, but to skate his way down the hallway on some glorious and invisible river of ice. By the time Miss D appears on this fateful day, however, Teddy White has been plucked off his ice and is hanging by his ear in a sixth-grade teacher's grip. Teddy's face has turned a ghostly white and there is a small but darkening wet spot on the front of his pants. As if to grant him mercy, even the meanest boys look away.

"Poof!" Miss D would sometimes purse her lips and fiercely blow toward us, and that was her blowing our fears away. "Poof!" She would blow into Sabrina Kaslov's ear when she became anxious about a math problem, or "Poof!" for Tommy Breen as he headed toward recess, and that would steel him for a battlefield of playground bullies. "Poof!" for Teddy White, when he suddenly faltered and could not swallow while reading aloud, and "Poof!" when his disconnected utterances seemed to sound the staccato pounding of his heart. It was a magic that we allowed from Miss D, if for no other reason than because it seemed to work.

Today, however, as we watch with horror and with pity as Teddy White swings from the grip of a sixth-grade teacher, Miss D's magic looks like tired antics to us. It seems to us now that the only help that Teddy White could get would be due punishment. He has, after all, clearly mistaken a school hallway for a river of ice. Even more to the point, Teddy White's due punishment would be our due process.

Due process at Johnson Elementary has always seemed to us the easiest of mathematical problems. It has always been the manifestation of some perfect ratio, some scale of justice, some division of angels among us—a division like the hierarchy of clergy that we understood so well, and like the different ranks of elementary school teachers that we learned to acknowledge. In spite of the happier results that Miss D's magic might have ushered in, we feel sadly confirmed in our reserve toward her today. Teddy White, we conclude, will become the poster child of Miss D's flawed teaching—a casualty of her altruism. We feel worlds apart from her.

All the more troubling for us is Miss D's persistence. When Miss D asks us why none of us has helped poor Teddy White and then straightens her back toward the sixth-grade teacher, she seems to forget not only the earthly hierarchies of elementary school teachers, but also the legions of angels that watch us and weep for us when we challenge these hierarchies. As far as we can tell, Miss D has crossed a line: she mistakenly chooses humanity over hierarchy—Teddy White over the rank of a sixth-grade teacher—and the hush in our school hallway is deafening. The last thing we see is Miss D bent over, her mouth near Teddy White's ear.

"Poof!" It is a gust of black magic—or it is unimaginable courage. It is the end of Miss D's teaching career—or it is the assertion of true teaching. It is the end of dreaming—or it is the storming of the Bastille. We are not sure which. Most of us bow our heads in fear of the sixth-grade teacher's fury. And we are stunned a second time when she does not challenge Miss D, but without a word loosens Teddy White from her vice grip.

"Poof! Poof! Poof!" The mean boys look oddly maternal

as they gather Teddy White up into their fold and make their way down the school hallway, at times twisting him into a headlock, at other times hoisting him above their waists and carrying him along with them as if on some wave of victory. "Poof! Poof! Poof!" they chant as they trip and skate and stomp their way toward the east stairway exit and out to the playground—jubilant in their new marching song, their new mantra.

Months later, when a patch of ice appears on our playground, Miss D would bring an old pair of ice skates to Teddy White. From our second-floor window, we would watch Teddy dash from side to side on a small, translucent patch of ice on the frozen playground below—tripping and recovering, and at times surprising us with his upright form and grace.

When John G. Ashe complains that the bell to end recess has rung long ago, Miss D says that none of us should feel cheated because this is something different from recess. "Something very different," she says leaning toward the window.

As much as we want to cling to our Old World Order, it becomes clear to us that we are in a New World Order now. We feel established hierarchies crashing all around us. The good children receive gifts, or stickers for their bicycles; the bad children receive gifts, or stickers for their bicycles. We are at a loss. As hard as we struggle to crack the codes of conduct here, the best that we can tell is that there are no codes—at least not familiar codes. Instead of detention, there is tomorrow: a new day, a new chance, a new you. Instead of branding, there is perpetual reinvention. Without our personal histories that we carry like preserved carcasses from first grade to second grade and from second grade to third, we will have to create new histories. Self-fashioning will become our central study.

❧

It becomes more and more clear to us that in Miss D's class, if we are going to learn anything, we are going to have to learn new rules of engagement. Lessons in fractions would not be simply lessons in fractions. When Miss D leans toward John G. Ashe, while the rest of us hobble through our math problems, and asks him "What's new?" she is hoping for an answer—not an answer to the math problem, but an answer to her question: Had he discovered his own shortcut to solving a problem? Had he found himself thinking outside the box? Had he uncovered even better questions than the ones in his thick and musty Level 4 math book?

Later, in the fifth grade, we will be punished for not showing our steps, for abridging at will the cumbersome stages of a multiplication or division problem. This year we would be applauded for it. In the spring of this year, when our team of Glen Rooney, John G. Ashe, Bailey Arnold, and Sabrina Kaslov earn first place in the Future Mathematicians & Problem Solvers Contest between grade four and grade five, John G. Ashe will congratulate himself again and again for leading the team with his "thinking outside the box." It will be the only time that the rest of us forgive John G. Ashe for his bravado and self-promotion.

What becomes more and more apparent to us is that Miss D has constructed for us her own conundrum: How to loosen us from the shackles of a public school education that favors standardized tests over non-standard lives? How to steer us toward immeasurable outcomes—without losing our allegiance, and without losing her job? Miss D's lessons will require us to think globally rather than cherish our parochialisms: a classical education for the woefully pragmatic children of a shipyard town south of Boston.

Education, for us, will be something that will happen without our parents' consent. Education will be insurrection: a dispensing of sanctioned attitudes, especially those attitudes that clip our most secret ambitions. A shedding of established caste systems and an imagining of new lives. *Children, how should I draw a hero?* This was a *coup d'état* that was taking place in Room 20, a face-off between the Old Guard and something new. As if sensing her feeling of being pressed for time, we follow Miss D's disposition toward the holistic, her preference for larger truths. The facts, she seems to imply, will take care of themselves.

They do.

August, 1984

A present—belated—(a something old) for your wedding: the handkerchief enclosed was given to me by a little boy the first year I taught school. I think he must have stolen it, which in my benighted state of mind, makes it all the more valuable.

Lovingly,
D

THE GOOD THIEF

John G. Ashe is reading aloud when our art teacher, Mrs. Foreman, appears in our doorway. She is round and breathless. Her flushed cheeks draw our eyes up to the wilted silk petunias on her straw hat, and then down again to the ruby snap-buttons on her boxy housecoat.

One by one, we have been called out of the classroom to be interrogated by her in the hallway, and now her scent seems to hang on our clothes and in the air. It is a dizzying scent, like a medley of Christmas samples from the perfume counters in department stores—rosehips, holly flowers, lavender, and apple blossoms.

It is our second week in France, and we are what Miss D calls *everything French*. The American flag in our classroom has been paired with the French Republic's stripes—stern and blazing primaries in blue, white, and red. For eight days in a row, Sabrina Kaslov has worn her uncle's French beret to school, and for eight days we have eaten lunches of bubbling cider, pungent cheeses and pâtés, baguettes, apples, and pears.

When Mrs. Foreman could not be with us last week, Miss D led our art lesson. At precisely the moment when Mrs. Foreman should have entered our classroom, Miss D leaped to her feet and asked us,

"Children! What *color* is this?"

It was a small cylindrical bottle that Miss D passed under our noses as she glided up and down our rows.

"Close your eyes!! Close your eyes!!

What color is...this scent?"

For what seemed like hours, we passed around seasonings from Miss D's kitchen, and we wrote down the color of cinnamon, the color of oregano, the color of mint. After a while, we forgot Mrs. Foreman's taxonomy of primary and secondary colors, and instead we painted palettes of seasonings all around us. At lunch time that day, over the scent of liver pâté and fresh pears, Miss D showed us a black-and-white photo of a handsome man with thin silky hair whose dreamy eyes seemed to see us—and then see through us.

"BO-DER-LAARRRRR-E"

Miss D's lips made a sensual oval, and then released a long and rippling breath, as if she were blowing smoke rings. We struggled to follow her smoke.

"BOW-DEEE-LAI-YERRRR"

We puffed out the mispronounced name with a new sense of chic. We seemed to be speaking in tongues as Miss D led us in a kind of chant or rhapsody of saying his name in parts:

"LARRRRRRRRRRRE
LAYER
    DER
DE
    DERLARRRRRRRRRRE
    DELAYER
Bau—de—laire"

We said his name backwards and forwards, until our lips were thick and trembling, until our tongues were no longer ours, and until our faces looked utterly French.

"Un homme de génie! A don! Un extraordinaire!"

Miss D sang these French words. They were words and phrases already on placards on our wall, words that we had now and then felt encouraged to attach to ourselves. A genius! A gift! Extraordinary! But, this day, these were clearly his traits, and our exercise in matching scents with colors was his lesson for us. An astonishing man with astonishing ideas, Miss D told us; he could be one source for our own dormant gifts. And according to Miss D, we were shockingly gifted: future astronauts, future sopranos, future poets, future painters, nurses, marathon runners, actors. We were all there.

John G. Ashe and Miss D are giving us their best performances today when Mrs. Foreman appears in our doorway and interrupts by pretending to clear her throat. We know that we should respond to Mrs. Foreman, but it is the storming of the Bastille that we are immersed in, and Miss D is causing a gust as she breaks down enormous invisible prison doors in the front of the classroom.

Mrs. Foreman clears her throat again. John G. Ashe stops reading, and Miss D stops breaking down doors. Mrs. Foreman tells John G. Ashe and the rest of us that *SHE* knows that *ONE OF YOU KNOWS* where her five dollars went. She leans into her words like a seer, and she dangles her straw purse from her forearm.

"What color is fear?"

We all straighten up. Miss D has seated herself and is looking over her own pleated skirt and picking off pieces of invisible lint.

"What color? What color is fear, darlings?"

Mrs. Foreman looks aghast as her eyes move from Miss D to all of us, and then back to Miss D.

"White, like a scared face!" Mary Wiles shouts out.

"Black, like a man," John G. Ashe chimes in.

A few weeks ago, Miss D had told us about a man from Mississippi who had forced a university to admit Black students too, and then he caught a shot in the back while walking home. "It wasn't just any walk home," Miss D told us, when that Black man fell dead from a shot in the back. He was making what he called his *March against Fear*.

"We must all march against fear," Miss D told us, and so we marched that whole week. While our peers played ball or jumped rope and innocently sang:

"Mi-ssi-ssi—and—a–ppi,"

some of us trotted in protest, double file across the playground. And at the end of the school day, on our trek home from school, we marched in protest along the unevenly paved sidewalks, The Busy People crowding us and falling into hedges and front lawns along the way. We marched not so much against bullets or racism, but against fears that we knew: we marched against belt marks on the backs of a girl's lily-white legs; we marched against codes that label us; we marched against the dead soul in whiskey; we marched against the relentless summoning of shipyard horns; and we marched against the brutality of fourth-graders by fifth-graders.

&

"Joy?"

Miss D is asking us to think like Baudelaire again:

"Green and red," Mary Wiles shouts, "like Christmas!"

"No! Joy is bright pink!" Sabrina Kaslov corrects her.

We are all in it now. Some of us are on our feet shouting out colors, others sit still and scan the array of hues all around us. Miss D continues to address us without looking up:

"What about anger—what color is that?"

"It's white!" Nicholas K. offers right away, "like a fist!"

And in the same breadth, he instantly corrects himself,

"No, it's red. Yeah, anger is red. Like poor old Tommy's face when the fifth-graders are done with him."

A few of the motherly girls exhale a collective sigh and turn in their seats to examine Tommy Breen. Miraculously, he has escaped the fifth-grader's bullying today. His pale and freckled face looks plumper and fresher than usual. When he smiles a crooked smile, the motherly girls all tip their heads to one side as if they have choreographed this especially for him, and Sabrina Kaslov even blows Tommy Breen a kiss.

Miss D seems to want to know more:

"And what does anger sound like?"

"A beating drum!" Mary Wiles shouts.

She is on her feet and excited by the game, but she quickly slumps back into her seat when Nicholas K. lets out a hoot of disapproval.

We sense that the game may be coming to an end, so we look toward Miss D for more. Miss D tips her head backwards and searches the ceiling for a word, for a human condition, for a moment in our lives:

"Loneliness?"

"Like nothing," someone instantly offers, as if this has been the easiest word of all, "Loneliness sounds like nothing."

"And it's white," someone else adds.

We all look at the redhead in the back of the classroom, the bruises on her ivory forearms showing beneath her blanched and crumpled blouse. "Extraordinaire," Miss D gasps, "Extraordinaire." And she bows her head. With her right palm she irons the front of her skirt—a gesture she saves for us. It is a gesture that says, "Well done," and we know that she has to look down or else our brilliance will blind her.

Mrs. Foreman is holding her ground. She announces that one of us must come forward this instant—or she will punish us all. We are genuinely confused. We look to Miss D for help, but she shrugs and smiles.

"Let's have a collection!" Mary Wiles shouts, "for the Good Thief!"

Weeks earlier, Miss D had read to us the story of "The Good Thief."

"What should happen to a thief?" Miss D asked us that morning.

"He should get the strap," Glen Rooney shot back from under his helmet.

Miss D pursed her mouth to that, the way she does when she is giving us time for a different answer. When the thief in the story did not get the strap but he did get Paradise, we remembered that. Miss D said that stealing does not make a man a thief, and we wondered what it made him then. That is up to the man, she said. Until his last breath, that is up to the man. Glen Rooney and a few of the other boys looked relieved to hear that.

Mrs. Foreman hovers in our doorway and looks out over our heads. Above her head, and above the door, are blue and red and white placards with the terms we have learned:

AMOUR   REPUBLIQUE   RESISTANCE

We look steadily at one another—not a thief among us—and then back at Mrs. Foreman. Within a few minutes we have repaid the thief's debt. We have filled a lunch bag with Saltines, a pear, and a handful of coins from our milk-money box. Mrs. Foreman glares at us.

We are communicants, but not in her parish. We are patriots, but not from her country. We are French. We are a Republic.

February, 1985

*Some nameless virus I've been fighting these past weeks has im-
mobilized my body and soul. I can take the physical inadequacies,
but to see and not feel is all the difference between living and existing ... I am glad that you are reading R.L.S. I know he isn't
the greatest writer, but there is something so human, and of the
present about his personality that my enthusiasm has never cooled.*

Lovingly,

D

THE MAGIC JACKET

It could happen at any time. In the middle of a thorny math problem. At the start of lunch. During morning announcements. She will drift off toward the narrow closet near her desk, then lift the jacket out slowly and slip her arms into it. She will do this with such a lack of self-consciousness that she might be slipping on her coat to go home. And for just a few moments, while she adjusts the jacket to her hunched and narrow shoulders, we seem to disappear. She is dressing for something important, and we can barely watch without feeling like intruders. Tattered and many-times mended around the collar, richly woven in mythical patterns, a tapestry of Gauguin's tropical flora, her jacket astonishes us with its ritual feel. It is less a jacket than it is a costume for ceremony.

The ceremony is story. We *shusssshhhhhh* ourselves quiet as she moves to the front of the classroom. Looking over our heads, she starts in a whisper as though talking to herself, or as if she is retracing her steps toward some lost object. We are the lost objects that she is looking for and the stories are always about us.

"There was a beautiful girl in braids—"

and our eyes race around the room for a girl in braids—

"who wanted nothing more than to go to—"

"Greece!" Nicholas K. yells.

"Italy!" someone else offers.

We are collaborators, finishing her lines, writing her stories—and with a rival spirit among us, we are writing our own stories, as well. We feel ourselves leaving port, leaving a shipyard town with its beautiful Irish and Italian and Greek and Portuguese men, who pour out of bars for their short treks home.

We feel ourselves crossing a bridge—any bridge—perhaps the Fore River Bridge with its industries like bookend dreams set in General Dynamics and Proctor & Gamble. Battleships or soap, it doesn't seem to matter what men make in our town, as long as they are promised a week's pay and the drone horn that releases them at the end of the day. From our schoolyard, we glimpse their tired shuffle home: the midnight shift returning home, bent and older than their years, almost too tired to carry their empty metal lunch boxes.

The magic jacket is our ticket out—to tropical and exotic islands certainly, and to Robert Louis Stevenson's Samoa inevitably. There, on Stevenson's verandah in Vailima, we dine with servants and with the native Samoans. A porcelain-skinned girl in braids; a wisp of a girl with belt marks on her legs; a jumbo-sized fourth-grader in his dead father's native Greek attire; a ten-year-old reclusive math champion in an astronaut's helmet; a daughter of the youth director at St. Jerome's Catholic Church; a son of a soul-dead alcoholic. All of us there on Stevenson's verandah, feeling with every turn of Miss D's pages, the breeze of the South Seas.

And while Miss D reads to us, some of us quietly shift from our chairs to the classroom floor: from verandah to the warmth of Stevenson's lush and sprawling lawn. After a while, it seems unnatural to look like ourselves anymore, so Miss D brings us new clothes.

"RLS would wear this!" Miss D announces, as she dons John G. Ashe in a silk scarf, "and Fanny this!" And the girl with bruises is suddenly ephemeral with a string of pearls around her neck.

There are boys' shirts with tight cuffs; and for the girls, there are long and cumbersome Victorian dresses. Some wear these pieces all morning, and as the second bell rings for math to begin and for lunch to end at Johnson Elementary School, we push our desks aside and sit on the floor to a beautiful native feast, just as Stevenson and his wife, Fanny, sat with the king of Hawaii in Honolulu. Though we eat from paper lunch bags, we might just as well be dining from coconut bowls full of raisins and nuts, sweet milk and tea.

"Imagine, darlings, how sick he was—and how brave."

It was Stevenson's battle with consumption that Miss D always meant, a battle with nature itself that somehow rendered him heroic to her.

"Imagine her heartache, and her passion!"

We are too young to imagine Fanny Stevenson's passion for a man so much her junior, too full of hope to imagine her decision to leave a husband and two sons for a consumptive poet and novelist. And we are too natively Irish and Italian and Greek and Portuguese to really grasp Miss D's attachment to the natives of Samoa.

But we do know about desire; and gradually, we are coming to know about the difference that leaving one place for another could make. We know about this in the realest of senses: we wear the clothes, we dine outdoors, and we feel the expanding of our own spirits and intellects that comes from putting on another man's mind.

To the principal glancing in, this is story hour and, although we are down on the floor rather than tucked neatly behind our desks, we are quiet and good. To us in our Victorian wayfarer clothes and to Miss D in her magic jacket, this is brave and rugged travel and we are emboldened pioneers—poles apart from our homelands, yet never more at home.

April, 1986

The trouble is, I am sure, that you never learned to be an apple polisher. Oh, and I hope you never will!

At your side,

D

CANDY CIGARETTES

When the principal asks us why we have been sent to his office, Sabrina Kaslov exhales in a matter-of-fact manner: "Smoking." She slides her No. 2 pencil out of its velvet sleeve and asks him, "Do we need to sign in?"

We are so astonished by Sabrina's temerity and her self-possession that not one of us steps up to correct the record. Or perhaps the record was right. Although our cigarettes had sugary red tips on them, we had, most definitely—and in the most romantic of meanings that we had gleaned from TV commercials—been smoking. We had been discovered by our art teacher, Mrs. Foreman, during outdoor recess; languishing on the sidelines and blowing out pretend smoke rings that yawned and hovered above us. We held the candy cigarettes between our two forefingers exactly the way we had seen our parents do it, but with the sophistication and celebrity-suave that we had seen on television:

Where dreams come true. This menthol is for you.

With each puff, we felt ourselves choosing the celebrity life. We sat with our backs against the school's cool bricks and we gazed out over the playground. The bricks were the backs of our lounge chairs on the deck of a luxury ship, and the playground's open field was the deep, expansive Atlantic. We were enjoying a good smoke as we sailed for Greece, or Corsica, or anywhere cobalt blue and warm.

We were smoking pals, travel mates, confidantes. Mary Wiles was the seductive Lauren Bacall with her ringlets of silky blonde hair and her ruby-red lips pursed around her slender white cigarette. "Got a light?" she would ask John G. Ashe, and John G. Ashe was suddenly Bogart as he flicked on his invisible lighter and she cupped her hand around his. Sabrina Kaslov was a young Betty Davis or some femme fatale, introspective and dark, as she pushed out the words between puffs of her doomed love affair with a fifth-grader named Richard Bliss. We knew that we would never look as glamorous as Sabrina Kaslov did in her Cossack hat and her fur-trimmed coat on this damp December morning, but we loved all this sorcery and play.

When Sabrina empties her box of Lucky Lights onto the principal's desk, a few of them break into pieces and we feel our luxury ship yaw and drift. When she takes one step backward to join us, we step backward too—not to leave her behind, but to cling to our listing lounge chairs, to save what we can, and to give up as little as possible.

A man is only as good as his actions.

It was a motto, polished, cut into brass, and framed in wood on the principal's desk—but we already knew the lesson. We knew it as the moral of a myth that we had read with Miss D. Miss D loved the myth and its message so much that she asked us to come up with a memorable phrase to remember it. When we did, she painted our phrase onto a poster board and then she posted it at eye level near our classroom door. On especially sunny days, while we waited impatiently in triple file to run down the hall to recess, we would let those words roll off our tongues. It was a way to count the seconds.

A. Man. Is. What. A. Man. Does.

A man. is. What a man. Does.

A man is. What a man. Does.

A man…

As we wait in the principal's holding room, we count the

seconds—A. MAN. IS. ONLY. AS. GOOD. AS. HIS. AC-
TIONS—and we somehow know that we are good. "Tall
and Small," Miss D used to say when she had a story's lesson
in mind. The lesson, she would mean, goes for adults as well
as for us children. It was an idea that continued to surprise
us: the idea that adults still learned lessons, and that all of
the lessons in the world were not just for us. And then, of
course, the logical conclusion: If adults were like us—forever reforming themselves—then they certainly could hold no
absolute power over us.

These were shocking ideas, so heretical that we kept them
to ourselves. When these ideas did surface now and then,
we did not speak them; instead, they surfaced through our
body language—a body language so shared, so communal,
that only we in Room 20 knew how to decode it. When a
substitute teacher made Mary Wiles miss recess to clean up
a mess that someone else made, we did not fear absolute
power. "Subs have it hard," Mary said, not with words, but
through her serene and freckled smile; and Bailey Arnold,
who did make the mess, stayed behind to help clean. "She'll
learn," Bailey said, not with words, but with a shake of his
head—but he did not mean Mary.

The principal is reminding us that we need to use our playtime
well, and that cigarettes are not for youngsters, not in life, not
at play, not…. Of course, he is right. From the look on Mary
Wiles's face, he might see that we even admire him for caring
for us. What he has overlooked, however, is the truer travesty
we committed today—our near escape. For all the reasons
we have to admire the principal today, we regret his short
view. Outside, the faint call of an empty swing creaks; a few
of us look up half expecting to see a luxury ship tack toward
the east. When we bow our heads again, it pleases the principal, but it is not for him. It is to see ourselves free: lovers

of luxury ships, sophisticated smokers, actors and actresses, ex-patriots, lovers of poetry, good thieves, escapees, makers of our own destinies. A. Man. Is. Only. As. Good. As.

We count the seconds, while we wait for the principal to deliver his sentence. We stand before him like candidates for conversion, and yet we have grown so unfamiliar with these us-and-them scenarios that we cannot help wondering: Who might be converted here—student or principal? Mary Wiles smiles as if in the presence of a different judge—something private and sacred. She is judging the judge. And perhaps because she stands closest to the principal, Sabrina Kaslov cocks her head and locks her gaze on him. *Tall and Small.* The refrain seems to ring in our ears, and we knowingly nod at her as our eyes move from the height of the principal's head to the top of hers. A. Man. Is. Only. As. Good. As. His. Actions.

In the distance, the Shipyard horn summons the second shift. Time. Work. Fathers. Whiskey. God. The bread and butter of our lives, a kind of contract with our god that the Shipyard's sounding horn has always reminded us of—a contract that the principal cannot be expected to know, but that we know.

In a whimsical moment during recess, weeks before, Mary Wiles surrendered to us: "Sometimes, I pretend that the Shipyard horn is our luxury ship! And at night, when I'm lying in bed, I pretend that the cars that pass over the Fore River Bridge are big waves. *Whooosh. Whooosh. Whooosh.*"

With each whooshing sound that she made, she waved her arms as though she were choreographing a fantastic production. We paused to see ourselves dancing on the main deck of our luxury ship. The rolling waves carrying us away. *Whooosh.*

The principal clears his throat as if to interrupt a conversation that we are having among ourselves. We look at him from our poses: a serene and forgiving smile, a shameless and cocked head, a phalanx of fourth-graders, not four feet tall, but high-minded and hopeful.

A man is only as good as his actions.

Mary Wiles's eyes dart from the motto to us, from us to the motto, and back to us. What actions will the principal take? We all wonder.

How. Good. A. Man. Is. He?

How Good. A Man. Is He?

How Good?

June, 1986

I loved your last letter so much that I put it away for special safe keeping, and though I had ransacked the house twice hunting for it, I didn't find it until today—safe within the pages of the Jerusalem Bible, no less, along with a fifteen-dollar rebate for my car insurance! The rebate was given because I'm supposed to be a safe driver. Alleluia for the first finding, and a triumphant grin for the latter.

Lovingly,
D

ORA ET LABORA

Ora et Labora. Pray and work. No matter what faith we arrive with, we learn the Benedictine way. Pray out loud and pray alone, Miss D tells us, and so, as if in accordance with seasons of faith that only we seem to know, we pray aloud and we pray alone. In a public school that still allows the open recitation of prayer, Miss D's spirituality does not alarm us. It is her concern for our individual lives that alarms us. We join her in prayer, at first to simply accommodate her; after a while, to do what prayer does—to offer her our fellowship. In the mornings, we pray aloud. We stand among our classmates and take our turns announcing our needs: intentions for a sister at home with measles, for a father who is out of work, for a dog hit by a car, for a cousin in Vietnam, for better grades in math.

We pray looking east and west. On Wednesdays, we read aloud from the New Testament and the Old Testament; and Sabrina Kaslov, whose confident voice somehow soothes us, will read from the Talmud. In the fall, there are Jewish blessings for apples and honey. In the spring, St. Francis's songs and stories of revelation and rebirth: Moses, Abraham, and Jesus. In the winter, there are walks through the snow to practice Buddha's eight ways: a walk through our playground, what Miss D calls our *pure ground*, to shake off our eight ways of suffering the way one might shake off old habits. No cold in our shoes, although the snow melts between our toes; no fear of ridicule, although our peers watch us from classrooms above; no sense of time, although the

133

school bell rings inside to a constant and absolute schedule.

We pray to renounce fear. "The Apostle's Creed," Miss D once told us, was a song of revolution sung one afternoon among hundreds in the middle of a Roman city by men whose knees must have been shaking. "Real prayers," she told us, are said "with shaking knees." And so before tests (especially math tests), some of us stand and stretch and feel our knees give out. For those with a god in our lives, as for those without a god, it is a time for letting in a kind of grace that our faiths or our natural world wants to give to us. A sprinter's stretching routine; a chess player's meditation before the match. As she scribbles math problems on the blackboard, Miss D calls out to us, over her right shoulder

"How are our knees, darlings?"

It is the part of our tests that we like the best, the moving and playing, but also the moment of reckoning. We have done our daily work and we have trusted ourselves. The rest is now up to our different gods, or our trust in the natural world.

"Have we done our best to prepare?"

The test that came before the test. In Miss D's class, this was perhaps the only test.

ORA ET LABORA

Emblazoned in glittering gold on a black poster board that hangs by the classroom doorway, this directive meets us at eye level when we work at our desks, waist-high when we stand to go out. Each time we leave our classroom, we touch the sign lightly with our fingers the way that players on a football team might brush their hands over a victory placard before going onto the field. We touch the placard for luck, for team spirit, for some sort of promise that we will carry our lessons onto the field.

And this is her goal: that our lessons will become our fieldwork. We know that we are the chosen ones because Miss D told us so, and we know from the start that we are not just preparing ourselves for any game, but for the big game, for the challenge of our lives—and that while victory takes some preparing for, we had better be ready as well for defeat.

March, 1987

Was it Gandhi who said it? Deep feeling—love especially—is reserved for the brave, since the coward is incapable of it.

Ever yours,

D

A PURPLE HEART

For the past two weeks Tommy Breen has been sporting a magnificently mutating black eye and a Purple Heart on his chest. A badge of honor that Miss D cut from a faux-suede cloth remainder in our art supplies box and then decorated with a strip of gold sticker stars, the Purple Heart seems to rest against Tommy Breen's chest like a superhero's shield.

According to a lesson that Miss D once delivered to us, George Washington established the Purple Heart Medal to honor the courageous and wounded in their fight against enemy forces. In his courage against fifth-grade bullies during recess, Miss D tells us during a quiet award ceremony over lunch, "The Honorable Thomas O'Malley Breen, fourth-grader at Johnson Elementary, showed us today that right beats might."

Right did beat might, but it was not easy to witness. Although the recess bell was buzzing, and he could have heeded our calls for him to jump into line with us, Tommy Breen had a different goal that morning. For the first time all year, Tommy did not run to us, he did not cry for help from the man-boy, Nicholas Kastinopoulos, and he did not seem to feel the repeated punches to the small of his back and to his slender and flaccid arms. Instead, he stayed behind while the rest of us stood silently at attention, frozen and horrified, suspended in the *hushhhhh* between the first and second recess bells.

Clouds that had kept their distance during recess now descended and seemed to envelop us. We recognized them.

These were the same clouds that enveloped Achilles in his battle with Hector. The will of the gods, Miss D had told us as she read the battle scene to us. And then, as if to deliver to us a wand that only we would know how to safely use, she leaned into our grid of desks-in-rows and sounded out the words with dramatic elocution: "Deus ex machina."

Although one of the teachers was directing us to file forward, we did not move. We could not move. The only picture that we could imagine was Tommy Breen's new Raggedy-Andy arms and head. The only sound that we heard was the terrible echo from the nearest corner of the schoolyard: the treble bass of choking blows.

Tommy Breen had not stood up to the fifth-grade bullies, as Miss D's speech would have us believe, but he had not exactly stood down either. When one of the toughest fifth-grade boys pushed Benjamin Bomberger, Tommy had simply stepped out of line to keep from falling too. It was a kind of two-step that Tommy and Benjamin had choreographed since the third grade.

Although Tommy Breen was one of the smallest fourth-graders, he still dwarfed Benjamin Bomberger, and so he became Ben's back. Whenever we assembled ourselves into rows for class photos, whenever we fell into line for recess, whenever we took our positions on the playground, Ben would squeeze in front of Tommy and into the arc of Tommy's slender and slightly hunched frame. While the rest of us forced a smile for a class photographer or while we stood sullenly in line at the end of recess, Tommy Breen would gaze over the top of Benjamin Bomberger's head and study the world before him—and for just that short time, Tommy Breen became taller and stronger than somebody else.

"Hey, Boooom-boy-gah!" It was Benjamin Bomberger's mother that the fifth-grade boys were mocking—an accent that, from the moment they heard it, they instantly con-

demned as barbarian, as attached to somewhere else—even
if that somewhere else were the not-too-distant neigh-
borhoods of Paterson, New Jersey. "Boygah" instead of
"berrgah"—the proper pronunciation in North Weymouth,
Massachusetts. Their mastery of her New Jersey dialect with
a German-Polish inflection might have won our praise had it
not cut such a visible wound through Benjamin Bomberger's
psyche. As the new kid who came to our school midyear,
Benjamin Bomberger was still catching up. He was still discovering the hierarchy at Johnson Elementary of fifth-graders over fourth-graders, of tall over small, of principal's son
over shipbuilder's son, and of cunning over kindness.

When the taunting began, Tommy Breen put his arm
around Benjamin Bomberger the same way that Nicholas
Kastinopoulos had done for Tommy on so many occasions.
He turned the two of them around with such stiffness and
calculation that they might have been synchronized skaters
lost in their own routine. It was as if the fifth grade never
existed, as if no one had ridiculed anyone's mother, as if they
had better things to do. Those of us who had been calling
to Tommy and Benjamin to join us in line sighed with relief
at this happy ending. But Tommy Breen was not the tall and
broad and muscular and prematurely hairy, heavyweight con-
tender that Nicholas Kastinopoulos was.

By the time Miss D and the principal got to us, all of the
fifth-graders had resumed their places in line. When the
principal tried to pass between Benjamin Bomberger and the
rest of us in order to reach Tommy Breen, we held our line
together as if someone had shouted, "Red Rover, Red Rover
send the principal right over!" Miss D asked us demurely
to please let the principal through, but we somehow knew
that she meant the opposite, and we squeezed one another's
hands even tighter than before.

Any minute now, we thought, Tommy Breen will pick himself up and take his place in line. Any minute now, we will all be returning to our classroom and Tommy Breen will slip off to the boys' room as he has done a dozen times before, and he will wash his face and hands, and he will straighten out his tangled jersey and he will flatten his disheveled and auburn hair, and he will check his sober and freckled face in the mirror the way one checks for something that he may have lost. Any minute now, all will return to normal, and so the principal should wait and see.

"What happened?" the principal wanted to know.

What happened was that the politics of the playground had suddenly shifted. Right faced Might, and from the looks of things, Right lost. What we would come to learn is that losses are not necessarily measured by injuries—but that victories always are.

"A Purple Heart," Miss D would tell yet another inductee later in the year, "for injuries while fighting the good fight." The good fight for Sheila McPherson had been her own private battle against an incapacitating shyness, a demon that struck her down during Wednesday Recitations, or that compelled her to sit alone in the classroom—mute and invisible, during lunch time. The injuries that Sheila McPherson had suffered were not as visible as Tommy Breen's, but according to Miss D, they were just as real. Sheila McPherson, Miss D confided in us, had suffered a broken heart—most likely, from the hailstorms of mockery from the fourth-grade boys: *Shhhhhhhhh—Sheila's here*, the fourth-grade boys would say, holding up their index fingers to their mouths the way that a librarian might when instructing us to be quiet. And then, as if to congratulate themselves for their high wit, the boys would double over with laughter, exulting in the fraternity that they exchanged for her self-hatred and isolation.

Yet, when on one dull November morning, in the middle of her Wednesday Recitation, Sheila curled up her nose and stuck out her tongue at a taunting Bailey Arnold, she turned her life around. "A Purple Heart," Miss D said, for Sheila's "decision to fight the good fight!" The implied message was that Sheila had something worth fighting for—something worth defending. She would have time enough after the fourth grade to discover what that something was. For now, for Sheila—as for the rest of us—the question was, *were we ready to fight?*

Noble wounds. Just battles. Purple Hearts. Honorable discharges. These would be concepts that we would learn in Miss D's classroom apart from the curriculum of our peers at Johnson Elementary. And so on that damp October morning, when we could not distinguish Tommy Breen's bloody lips and nose from the burnished tips of fallen leaves, when it looked like the fifth-grade bullies had clearly had enough of Tommy Breen—we knew better. Tommy Breen was just getting started.

In the thick of the bullies' jeers and jabs, he was rounding a corner in his life. He was going to stay the duration this time.

No choking calls for help.

No river of tears.

No terrified look in his coal-black eyes.

Just a steady and burning gaze at his opponents that would hopefully sear their consciences—a fiery gaze that would leave them branded in precisely the manner that they had tried to brand him. Tommy Breen knew exactly what he was doing. He was facing the enemy. And this time, the enemy would not be his wounded self.

Tommy Breen was looking for a medal.

"What happened?" The principal had assembled us to report to him. What happened was that a government of fear had been toppled. Without any dread of a tooth for a tooth, without any thought about tomorrow's recess, Tommy rallied to the principal's questions like a paid informer.

Suddenly bulletproof, he boldly pointed to the pack of fifth-graders who had collectively crippled him, who had made him wish that his own baptism had never happened. And, as if intending for Miss D and the principal and all the sky gods to be sure of the cruelest bully's name—as if for all of us to know our names—Tommy stared down a tall, broad-shouldered, and black-haired fifth-grader. Pointing to him with his trembling finger and bruised arm, his usual stutter a kind of foamy slur now, he named him:

"Sss-son-of-a-bitch!" he exclaimed.

The principal wanted Tommy Breen expelled.

Miss D wanted him decorated.

As if nothing could be clearer in a court of justice, we soberly fell in line to return to our classroom, eager for the ceremony to begin. The opening drum of our palms on the tops of our laminated desks that morning—good theater that Miss D joined in on—would become a kind of pulse for us, a recollection of a village song, a foundation in natural law that would carry us through a series of tyrannies both on the playground and in our workplaces for years to come.

October, 1987

You say I have convictions. I have now—but it took me so long. I don't think I truly believed in God until the first October Saturday of 1961. I made all the acceptable gestures, by rote, through fear maybe, or gratitude, but never with complete conviction until that morning. Nothing particular happened—as nothing particular ever seems to be happening—when we glimpse what we are made of.

All my love,

D

MODERATO

M*oderato.* A little slower than *allegro.* A little faster than *andante.* A moderate tempo. That, at least, is how the *Sanctuary* defines it. In the fourth grade, we know the word on a variety of levels. Moderato is one of the many words that we learn when Miss D sings with us. There is also *vibrato,* the rhythmic fluctuations in tone that we could create and that would give energy and life to a song. This is not to be confused with a *wobble.* There is Nicholas K.'s beautiful *soprano* voice, and Mary Wiles's *sotto voce.*

But moderato is the word that is posted on a wooden paperweight on Miss D's desk:

MODERATO

in brass plate letters with tiny screws that hold the letters to a dusty wooden block. It is her private prayer, not meant for us directly, since the word faces Miss D and not us. And yet, when we visit her desk, our eyes inevitably fix on the word while she labors over a paragraph we have written, or while she reviews the logic of our math problems.

Moderato. A moderate tempo. If this is Miss D's word, then it does not describe Miss D's pulse so much as it seems to recommend one—one that even she cannot always embrace. Along with a whole range of emotions that make her real to us, Miss D has a temper, which she lets us see now and then. And she invites us to have tempers too. Thus, the door in our classroom that leads to the fire escape is also the door to our Shouting Space. Since the fire escape stairwell is all but soundproof, we have Miss D's permission to escape to it at any time during the day for a good stomp or for a fierce, cathartic shout.

Not everyone views the Shouting Space as necessary. Sometimes, in the middle of composition hour, when the room is so quiet that we can hear our own pencils etching our thoughts into sentences and into imaginary worlds, Bailey Arnold or one of The Busy People will suddenly leap from his chair and rush past Miss D at the blackboard, and dart out for a shout, where he will playact uncontrollable wailing. After a while, when it becomes apparent to Bailey Arnold that Miss D is not going to come after him, he will return to the classroom exclaiming, "Whew!" and passing his hand across his forehead, and pretending at great emotional relief—catharsis as he has never known before.

Others see the Shouting Space as a right and natural outlet: when Nicholas K. does not like his math scores, we hear him through the thick fireproof door complaining in his native Greek like a distant and sad opera. And when Miss D does not like our laziness in our lessons; or when she can no longer tolerate our complacency when there are, as she says, higher mountains to climb; or when she cannot help but bristle at our contentment to settle for less, she will seem to collapse in front of us: her body still standing, but her head bowed low enough for her chin to touch her chest, shoulders caved in, and she will make a direct exit to the Shouting Space. Between her muffled gasps, we wonder at our desks how to win her back, though we know from our own visits to the Shouting Space, and from her previous happy returns, that this is not about us. The Shouting Space is where one leaves the others so one can look inside oneself.

For Glen Rooney, the Shouting Space becomes a kind of hospice. From fall through spring, on what seems like every Friday afternoon, just after cleanup time and just before school dismissal, Miss D and the rest of us routinely find ourselves standing in line and waiting patiently for Glen

Rooney to return from what seems like his regular stomp-and-shout session. Glen's mother died at the start of our school year, and Miss D said that weekends are hard without a mother.

From the fire exit landing, Glen's grief sounds out eerie echoes: a din of broken syllables and outbursts that raise up the hair on our necks. At other times, muffled sobs that make us imagine that his mother is there with him, rubbing his soft white hair and cradling him in her angel's arms. "Moderato," Miss D seems to whisper to herself or to us as we wait in line for Glen. We wait for Glen past the principal's dismissal announcements. We wait for Glen past Officer Kelly's safety advice. We wait for Glen past the purring of the groundskeeper's lawnmower below us.

On the days when there seems to be no end in sight, one of the motherly girls will tap on the fire escape door, slip through a tiny opening and draw Glen back to us under her arm. Each time they reemerge, she will shake her head at the other motherly girls as if to confirm our hunch: *No angel out there.* Sufficiently quiet for the fifth-grade teacher that escorts us, we will file down the halls of Johnson Elementary and outside into the day's bright light. As our eyes adjust, we will watch Glen's small form start its trek toward a motherless home again. Go moderately. Whatever directions Miss D gives us this year, they inevitably blend with the sign's recommendation:

MODERATO

A kind of prayer, or proviso that welcomes the whole being with all of its grief and anger and innocence and fear, and that gives it a shouting chamber to clear the heart and mind—and from which to come back one day, a little more whole and healing.

June, 1988

I took a course last week in Juvenile Writing. It was almost a spiritual experience and I alternated between suicidal depression and sheer happiness. The teacher said I was "identifying with my subject." Indeed.

So much love,

D

OPEN LINES

For virtually every assignment that we do—science experiments, math problems, composition, geography—Miss D asks us to move our pencils down several spaces—and then start.

"Start near the middle, darlings, near the middle!"

It is a technical request, the kind of request that we have grown accustomed to following with other teachers and without much explanation. But this time Miss D tells us that we should study the blank, open space at the top of our papers because that, she says, is the real assignment. We will need these open lines, she tells us, for our great ideas.

With a kind of perfunctory and tolerant attitude, we fill the space—but not with great ideas. Some of us make requests for new seating assignments. Others ask technical questions about the assignments at hand: "How long should this essay be?" and "May I have extra time after school to finish my math quiz?" Sabrina Kaslov writes notes with numbered questions, and always asks Miss D to *RSVP ASAP*.

After a while, however, these open lines look like slender arms reaching out to us and wanting some sort of embrace. Some of us use the space to share writing ideas with Miss D—ideas, which she will develop into whole pages with us. For others, these are open lines of a different sort: a place to share what's happening at home, or to ask Miss D questions about her home.

Nicholas K. keeps in his desk a drawing of her home that Miss D once sent to him. It was a picture of a small Cape

Cod–style house with a garden bursting with lilies—giant, robust lilies that dwarfed the quiet little house and that threw all perspective into question. And below the scene, a note that Miss D had written to Nicholas K:

I live near a garden that God grows.

Nicholas K. shows the drawing to all of us, and he must have asked Miss D for more details because often his graded assignments come back with more flowers: freshly picked daffodils strung together with a wisp of magic marker and hanging from the K in his name, or a bouquet of yellow and lavender pansies embroidered into the margins of his high-scoring math quiz like a monk's glosses. Nicholas K. holds these papers up high so that the rest of us can see them the way one might display good news to friends and competitors.

We look forward to Miss D's replies. They come to us with happy- and sad-faced stickers, with brilliant gold medallions, or with extra paper—because, as she says, great novels require paper. In fact, the assignment at hand often seems incidental to some other larger assignment—and these other assignments are so bold, so unique, so private, so personal, and so ongoing. Through our notes, we grow our own deep connections with Miss D. We come to know her in our various ways, and we are astonished by her various ways of knowing us.

Out of these exchanges come new names for us—and new possibilities. *Sir Charles* for the boy who loves history; our *Noble Greek* for Nicholas Kastinopoulos; *Steady Teddy* for the quiet contemplative boy; *V. G.* (*Veegie* to us) for the auburn-haired artistic boy whom Miss D calls *Van Gogh*; and *Heidi* for the girl who scribbled a salutation across the top of a math quiz, "Hi D." They are names, like so many of these new names among us that seem to yoke two impulses: Miss D's and ours. There is a sense in the air that everything is a work in progress. As long as we begin in the middle, no idea is ever locked in. As long as there is room on the page for thinking differently, no math problem that is solved the learned way is ever really solved.

When we advance to fifth grade, we miss these open lines; and anyone among us in that fifth-grade class can see which of us had been Miss D's students the previous year. We are the ones with our shoes off under our desks; the ones checking our knees and passing peppermints before a math quiz; the ones who, like members of the United Nations, seem to dress symbolically—a Greek silk shirt, an Irish lace collar on a plaid dress, a French beret. And, during essay writing, we are the ones crossing out and erasing whole lines of our work, as if to carve out some open lines. We are the ones revising and retooling, turning our papers over and then to the front again—looking down, looking up, looking for the open range.

PART III

Another Fall

May, 1989

So happy about your last day. Different from mine!

Your loving teacher and pupil,

Miss D

MIXED NUTS

Although I am twenty-four, she serves me Twinkies and a glass of milk. I am at her retirement home, as she jokingly calls it—a traditional cottage in the Cape town of Brewster. Since her retirement from teaching, she and her sister, Ruthie, have consciously designed it for their continual flow of guests: sitting rooms lined with books, end tables draped with the *New York Times Book Review* and the *Catholic Worker*, folding TV tables that spring open for nomadic types. It is a replica of her home that I used to visit in my earlier years—and in so many ways these visits continue to replicate our original bond.

On my twenty-fifth birthday, we will both sip sherry with Twinkies, as if at once savoring and grieving a coming of age. "Milk," she will say to me, "tasted so much better with Twinkies. Should we switch back to milk or move on to mixed nuts?"

We move on.

❧

When she throws her arms around me to greet me, I can hardly hold on to the extra-large can of mixed nuts that I have brought. "Okay, darling!" she exclaims. while still hugging me. "Let's crack open that sherry!"

Her warmth strikes a welcome contrast to the coolness that I have felt from some of my teaching colleagues and even from my own father these last few months. Although union-bred and union-brand, I have always dragged my feet in signing on with local chapters of the teachers' union for reasons that even I am not sure about, and that I hope she will help me to understand. Before I learned to read and write, I learned at my father's kitchen table that organized labor unions are the life-support system for the laborer; that unions give the laborer a voice, a forum, a family; that unions are the safety net for men who climb the sides of mammoth ships, for men who lay roads, for men who die young. But, since the start of my teaching career, I cannot see what the teachers' union has to do with shaping the minds of my students. I have found myself vacillating between a cool indifference and a cinema-style paranoia regarding the issue. I imagine colleagues gathering around yet another line in a contract that I have not signed, pointing to the empty line. I feel sure that she will help me sort through all this, but when I mention it to her, she seems to not really hear me.

"Politics are messy," she simply says. And, when she asks me, instead, if I have seen Seamus Heaney's latest collection of poetry, I am sure that I have offended her. For as long as I have known about political divides, I have imagined that she must be a Democrat and loyal to the core principles of her party, but what do politics have to do with this? I am wounded to think that politics might somehow sever our friendship. I am immobilized to think that she will not even discuss this with me. At dinner, I am quiet and heavy.

When did the fourth grade end and this afterward begin? In her fourth-grade class, I was the ten-year-old girl in pigtails, who preferred to answer questions only when called upon. *Heidi*, she named me. I was the one who scribbled the salutation *Hi D!* across the top of an almost-certainly-failing math quiz. It was an effort to earn her grace and an attempt to remind her that I did not fail in school subjects. A day later, the math quiz came back to me with a shimmering gold medallion sticker and a velvet purple ribbon attached to it.

Sure that it was not my exam, I began to hand it off to Glen Rooney, the smartest boy in our class—until I saw the note in her perfect script across the top of the page:

For Heidi - F Congratulations!!! You joined the human race!

When I showed it to my parents, they wanted to know what the joke was, and there was talk about Miss Dunning, and they would bring it up at Meet Your Teacher Night. Although I could not decode the joke, I felt sure I had scored the highest in a subject worth knowing—perhaps a subject that we had not covered yet, or that we would learn in the coming grades. I tacked the failed test to the bulletin board in my bedroom reserved for prizes and accolades.

In the fifth grade and sixth grade, I became a self-appointed ombudsman reporting to anyone who would listen—friends, parents, neighbors, but never, for some reason, Miss D—the unnaturalness of our new teachers. How Miss Diamond, our fifth-grade teacher, held our small button chins with her forefinger and thumb, and left the crease of her painted thumbnail there when we didn't speak up—or look up, or sit up, or quiet down. How we sat at our desks in rows doing drills and answering questions in workbooks; how our new teacher cherished silence and bristled when we spoke. How we tiptoed our way through a government of our thoughts, wary of missteps. How Tommy Breen stuttered his worst that year. How Mrs. Rogers, our sixth-grade teacher, threw a *Level 6 Civics* book at Bailey Arnold for reasons none of us ever learned—despite a week of conferences on the playground during recess.

Miss D had encouraged us to fight brute force with the force of reason. "Make reason your sword," she would tell us, "and the gods will favor you." But when Bailey Arnold drew from his pocket his own arsenal of marbles and rubber bands and confidently displayed them for Mrs. Rogers, telling her that these made better missiles than a *Level 6 Civics* book, the gods covered their eyes in fear.

I imagined a grand trial, not against me or my peers in the fifth and sixth grades, but against the fifth-grade and sixth-grade teachers themselves. They would stand and hear the charges brought against them:

Tired repetition of lessons
Obedience to the standardized test
Suspicion of the non-standard life
Inability to see the child standing before you
Love for uniformity
Disdain for the non-conformist

Even then, the act of turning books into projectiles seemed incidental next to these other inexpungible crimes. During my years in fifth and sixth grade, I would find reasons to casually pass by Miss D's classroom door and look in. If we happened to meet eyes, I would simply look back blankly at her as if to let her know that she had somehow defaulted on her promise. The Enlightenment was over.

As if to assure me that nature's laws were still our laws, she would smile at me from behind the Big Ideas Book on the corner of her cluttered desk and hug me without leaving her seat.

In my sixth grade at Johnson Elementary, Miss D chose me to be her "classroom monitor." It was a prized position at our school and it granted me—more than anything else—a chance to revisit her. During fire drills, I herded her students down and then up the sheer and whirling stairwells of Johnson Elementary. I escorted her students to the playground and to assemblies. I wore her Magic Jacket that she donned for storytelling, and I read Robert Louis Stevenson to them while they ate their lunches and while Miss D handed out chocolate mint patties. For these, and for other menial duties, she awarded me at the end of the year the Badge of the Miraculous Twelve-Year-Old Teacher and my own edition of Stevenson's *Treasure Island*. In the eighth grade, I brought her my own poems. In the Month of Famous Poets, she asked me to read aloud one of my poems to her class. "My children thought that poets were always dead," she confided in me later. "I had to set them straight."

In the awkward years of high school, I bicycled the long trek from my home and the saltwater air of North Weymouth to her book-filled home and the Colonial-estate ease of East Weymouth. Like rites of passage, the landmarks of North Weymouth disappeared behind me as I bicycled to her home—past the scent of frying oil at Wrye's Fish n' Chips; past the stained-glass windows of St. Jerome's Church, with its mysteries in multicolored glass that in just the right light during Mass washed over me in my pew like a warm bath. "No baptism better than that," Miss D told Nicholas K. one day when the afternoon sun suddenly poured through our row of windows and blinded him at his desk.

As early as our first year at Johnson Elementary School in North Weymouth, we learned that Weymouth is divided into four distinct townships—North, South, East, and lastly, a crossroads of a town called Weymouth Landing. Each township has its own character. North Weymouth: my township; blue-collar and briny; shipbuilders, welders, electricians; Wessagusset Beach, where we swim in a bay and sit on a beach wall and kiss our first kisses at night. Passing through North Weymouth, like a central artery, is Route 3A. Part boulevard, part barrier to the sea, part conduit linking the inhabitants of this coastal town to the city of Boston, it runs along the edges of our backyards and offers us everything we need: two pubs, two churches, a bakery, a drug store and soda fountain, a sewing machine repair shop; a fish and chips shop, a candy store, and a new ABC liquor store that our parents called the *package store*, as if it were a toyland of wrapped gifts.

A world apart from North Weymouth is Miss D's town— East Weymouth. These are the other people; a bedroom community of doctors, lawyers, and businessmen; the seat of government, Weymouth Town Hall; lush, green hills with sprawling Victorian and Colonial Revival homes. Inevitably, bicycling the long route from my home in North Weymouth to Miss D's home in East Weymouth, I felt like a defector. Landmarks like milestones or ruins leaned toward me as I pedaled past them and on to her house: the foreboding palm of the palm reader's shop; the long afternoon shadows of Johnson Elementary School; the cool and indifferent white-paneled doors of the First Congregational Church; the historic graveyard, where Abigail Adams's parents laid buried—like lovers arm in arm our school teachers told us— and where our own parents purchased their joined burial lots apparently as part of their wedding preparations.

"When I die, I know exactly the song that I want for my funeral!" Miss D once announced to our fourth-grade class. A few of us looked up from the Egyptian mummies that we were dressing for a school display. Without any prompting from us, Miss D broke into a marching demonstration:

O, When the Saints Come Marching In!

O, When the Saints Come Marching In…

I remember humming her funereal march on my walk home that day, my blonde pigtails bobbing from side to side as I imitated Miss D's joyful and final march. I imagined the parade of horns and trumpets that would exit the church. Miss D's grand finale—and mine too, somehow.

"Do you know Thoreau, darling?" she asks me after dinner, as she hands me a thin and tattered book. I politely flip through the pages. Page after page, her comments are scribbled in a feverish pencil in the narrow and yellowed margins. I see that I am eavesdropping on a conversation that she could not have intended for anyone except herself and Thoreau.

"Page fifty-seven, darling. How does that go?"

I read the passage aloud to her as I have in the past, when she has asked me to read something already committed to her memory.

I was not born to be forced. I will breathe after my own fashion.

I look up. She has closed her eyes, as she would in the fourth grade, so that she could hear our pure voices. She is nodding, as if in agreement with what I am reading, or as if to confirm that what I am reading matches her memory of this passage.

When I meet a government, which says to me, "Your money or your life," why should I be in haste to give it my money?

I pause for a few seconds to steady my voice. I see that we are talking politics. I see that I am swimming in her life and she in mine, and it takes all I have to stay on task.

I perceive that, when an acorn and a chestnut fall side by side, the one does not remain inert to make way for the other, but both obey their own laws, and spring and grow and flourish as best they can, till one, perchance, overshadows and destroys the other. If a plant cannot live according to its nature, it dies; and so a man.

I let my eyes wander over the words that she has underlined with a heavy pencil:

Obey their own laws...live according to its nature.

The words resonate like phrases that she would sometimes lift out of a story that we had read, and then post all around our fourth-grade classroom.

"How about that," she would whisper to us, as she smoothed down the last taped corner; and she would step back to study the words that she had taped to the wall of our fourth-grade classroom, her hands on her hips, head tilted and taking it in. The majority of us would tilt our heads too, as we studied her new graffiti. Sabrina Kaslov would inevitably complain that the left corner or the right corner was too high or too low. Over the next several days, many of us would embroider the words with our own swirling or geometric designs, and it never once occurred to us that ideas from books should be anywhere else but on the walls around us, like backdrop to the staging of our lives.

When I look up from the book in my hands, she seems to be napping. The afternoon's blue winter light cools the top of her bowed and blonde head, until the coolness seems to rouse her.

"To acorns!" she announces, as she straightens up, and we raise our glasses of sherry toward one another as if we are making a toast—or a promise—to live our own lives, to live according to our own natures, to obey our own laws, to flourish in our own light.

August, 1989

I've been reading all about Ireland, tracing and retracing our trip. And yet I think so much these days of that recluse E. Dickinson, who knew the world without leaving her room... There are so many ways to travel, aren't there?

Ever yours,

D

CULTURES CROSSING

It is Cultural Awareness Month at Harvard. As I lumber across the campus, my backpack slowing me down, I let two fellow grad students glide past me. Peeking out from under canopies of brilliant October leaves and at virtually every intersection on campus are octagonal-shaped pedestrian signs, yellow with black letters announcing the notice:

CULTURES CROSSING

A burst of wind suddenly strips a cluster of leaves from a bowing elm, and I am happy for a reason to stop and watch. Instead of falling leaves, however, I see Sabrina Kaslov chasing her uncle's rust-colored beret when the wind suddenly steals it from her head and sends it wheeling across the schoolyard of Johnson Elementary. Instead of whirling funnels of fall colors, I see Sabita Chadha's sari spiraling to the playground's hardtop in a game of Red Rover. "Red Rover, Red Rover, Send 'Bita right over," and as she runs toward us, her silken sash slips from her shoulders to the ground: golds, reds, and greens as vibrant as the Rajasthan desert at sundown. I see a ribbon of green Irish lace loosened from its bow in Mary Wiles's hair and twirling around her fingers while she wrestles with a math problem. What shaped the past is what shapes the present. And as I nod a hello to a student dressed in the customary black of Harvard students, I see Miriam Cohen's black accordion-pleated skirt flutter above her thick knees. A gust catches his dandyish white scarf, and I see cords of ivory: embroidered stripes down the front of an oversized cotton shirt that Nicholas Kastinopoulos wore like an ancient Greek tunic—remainder from his dead father's closet.

LIVING SOULS BLENDING

Or at least that was how we understood it then: multi-personalism, rather than multi-culturalism, since for Miss D the person preceded the culture. Indian. Greek. Italian. Portuguese. Russian. Irish. Lebanese. Buddhist. Catholic. Jewish. Protestant. All emerged in our classroom that year, but not during multicultural fairs or through federally funded programs. From its beginnings in the 1800s, the Quincy Fore River Shipyard had summoned hardworking men from many countries. Men with strong, calloused hands and broad chests. Men with bowed heads, chiseled faces, and—when they looked at their children—men with sad and watery eyes, eyes that seemed to look inward rather than at the moving world around them. We were a shipyard culture, and while we lived side by side, house by house, with one another, we saw ourselves as no more diverse than the ships that our fathers built—from freighters to battleships to aircraft carriers to submarines to LNG tankers.

In Miss D's class, we would come to see that beyond those ships, beyond our similar faces and similar lives, was a world of difference, but that these differences were best understood one person at a time. "One at a time," Miss D would tell us, when we banded together against another playground faction to tell our side of the story. "One at a time," when we paired ourselves up for an open-class quiz. And on the day when Miss D discovered us calling on our long-established legions—legions formed after four years on the same playground—in order to wage war against newcomers to our school, she bowed toward our bowed and ashamed heads. "We greet strangers with love," she whispered, "one at a time." There was a tiredness and a lack of compromise in her voice that we had not heard from her before.

When Sabrina Kaslov sadly informed us one day that her grandmother had uncovered a curse on her, we learned about culture. A slight and hunched Russian woman, whose flushed face peeked out from under a swaddling of cloth remainders, Sabrina's grandmother ran the palm reader's shop that we passed each morning on our way to school. Squeezed between a twenty-four-hour laundromat and a tobacco and cigar shop, it was a narrow and opaque windowfront. As if hidden by permanently drawn curtains, the interior of the palm reader's shop was concealed by a collage of advertisements, public notices, and newspaper clippings that covered the glass window from the inside. Desperate to see inside, we would press our noses to the glass and peer through the translucent poster of a Lucky Strikes ad, or jockey for a position where a sliver of Scotch tape met the glass.

What tipped us back onto our heels, and what lifted our chins and our gaze was the giant poster above all of these clippings. On a black poster board, with gold and silver sticker stars all around its frame, was a poster of an enormous palm. Bloodless and pearly white with vertical and horizontal lines drawn through it, The Palm stretched open and its four fingers pointed to the four planets—one planet for each finger: index finger/Jupiter, middle finger/Saturn, ring finger/Apollo, and baby finger/Mercury.

We had walked past The Palm so many times that by the fourth grade we knew this catalogue of fingers and planets by heart; and although we did not understand its meanings, we were drawn to its mysteries. On warm and lazy mornings, we would stand in front of the palm reader's window and compare The Palm to our own palms:

"I have two marriage lines on my hand."

"That means you will marry twice."

"No, it doesn't. Look, your lines are shorter than The Palm's."

"So?"

"So, that means you will ALMOST marry twice, but you'll NEVER marry."

"My lifeline is shorter than The Palm's."

"That means you will die young."

In spite of threats from Mary Gillis's mother that she had better not see us there again, four out of five days on our trek to school we stood before The Palm in the early morning light and we drank in The Palm's message. After several minutes, with our futures decoded by The Palm, we would bow our heads and quietly walk the rest of the way to school. Since marriage was not in the future for Mary Gillis, she would give up the idea of romance with the red-haired fourth-grader who had been kept back one year; and since longevity was not in the future for Mary Wiles, she would live that day like it was her last.

We came to revere and resent The Palm as much as Sabrina Kaslov must have. When Sabrina fought for her position on the playground, when she washed her tear-streaked face in the girl's room, when Miss D hushed us during lunch so that Sabrina could say her blessing—her *bracha*—over her turkey sandwich, we learned about culture. Because we loved Sabrina, we answered Sabrina's demands and we pitied her newly cursed soul. When Sabrina's grandmother cracked the curse of her granddaughter's life, and then sent her back to us—mired in a personal history, and hopeful for something better—she unwittingly cracked the curse of the whole lot of us.

&

When a fifth-grader called Louis DeGravio a *dirty guinea*, we learned about culture. The fifth-grader knew what he meant, but he sent Louis and the rest of us on a mad word hunt. For two days, we paddled through the pages of the *Sanctuary*.

"G-i-n-n-y. Ginny."

"It's not here."

"It says Gin, but not ginny. It's a card game. Gin rummy."

"A dirty card game? He said dirty Ginny."

"I guess so."

"Maybe he said gurney."

"Yea, the thing with wheels. My dad got one in the hospital."

"Yea, a dirty gurney."

"Why did he call Louis a dirty gurney?"

When Miss D explained the word to us that the fifth-grader had said, it was impossible for us to grasp. A gurney, at least, had wheels and a bed that rolled. But, the fifth-grader's word had nothing like this: no material substance, no proper definition in the *Sanctuary*. And what did Louis DeGravio have to do with such an ancient and residual hatred?

"Nothing," Miss D answered us, with a firmness that we were not accustomed to. "Louis was here first."

Louis was, indeed, here first. He had come into our lives long before the concept of culture had. And he was clean, not dirty at all. And his torso made a beautiful V-shape when all the other fourth-grade boys were still a capital I-shape, and he had flawless olive-colored skin, and burnt sienna eyes—and Mary Wiles, in spite of the short line in her palm, was in love with him. Mary Wiles fell in love with Louis De-Gravio before she changed the look of her hair, before she started painting her fingernails, before she wore her sister's T-shirt to school with its Italian flag on the front and with the advertisement for Anthony's Pizza on the back. Mary Wiles fell in love with Louis DeGravio before she fell in love with his culture.

When, one gray and cold day in November, John Paul Ambrose III slipped into our classroom minutes before the end of our school day, without a glance our way, without a fantastic story to excuse himself, and without a change of clothes from the day before, we learned about culture. In the culture of alcohol that etherized so many of North Weymouth's fathers and mothers, a few of us fared worse than others. A few of us learned, early in life, the cultural signs: a highball glass berthed in a pool of its own perspiration; a paper napkin with multiple folds and undecipherable doodling, like the soul-dead hieroglyphics that men leave behind for the living; a quart-sized bottle of whiskey left on a breakfast table like a sculptural companion to a box of Cheerios. Sleep inducers that made our mothers forget to wake up in the morning; forget to launder our clothes; forget to make our lunches; and after a while, forget to make excuses.

Through the politics of the playground, we had learned by the fourth grade the supreme happiness that comes with inclusion and the insufferable pain that comes with exclusion. But, it would be during Miss D's People Around the World lesson that we would hear for the first time that ostracism was no longer a death sentence. In fact, she would suggest, it is a badge of honor.

After commissioning our help to build a cardboard door that prevented us from passing through to Camelot, she posted a ready-made sign on the door:

WITTENBERG CASTLE CHURCH

It was the church, she told us, that showed Martin Luther what Martin Luther was made of.

"For some of us there is no church!" Miss D shouted to us, huffing and puffing as she nailed Martin Luther's *95 Theses* to her makeshift door. From our seats, we sat stunned by her blasphemy. We listened to Miss D read aloud Luther's protests against the Roman Catholic Church:

Graces of Pardon cannot be bought!

From the sweat on her brow, we imagined Luther's danger and we tasted the anger of Luther's church fathers. From earlier lessons, we could now envision the creative punishments of the Roman Empire. We imagined Miss D as food for the lions—or worse yet, alive, but despised. Intimidation. Ostracism. Exile. These were the choices that Martin Luther faced in our fourth-grade lesson. These were the only choices that we could imagine for Miss D in her role as a dissident monk that day.

Weeks later, when Bailey Arnold and Timothy Martin were accused of taping a list of handwritten complaints to the front doors of Johnson Elementary, Miss D took an unusual stand. This time she wanted names.

"Who were Luther's followers?"

"Lutherans," John G. Ashe quickly replied.

"Did Luther hide from the church fathers?"

"No," Timothy Martin seemed to whisper.

"Should these boys hide from their school principal?"

"No," Timothy Martin still whispered.

After the event, Timothy Martin would reclaim his title among the other teachers as one of the *bad apples* of Johnson Elementary. In Miss D's eyes, however, he became a paragon of courage and new ideas. For the rest of the school year, she would address him not as Timothy Martin but as *Reverend*, or *Doctor*, or *Headmaster*.

"I'm looking forward to that school that you will build some day," Miss D said, smiling at Timothy Martin after the principal's office and the Roman Empire had delivered their sentence of punishment.

Intimidation. Ostracism. Exile. These were the choices that Timothy Martin faced in Miss D's lesson and these were the choices that awaited the protester in so many venues, so many classes—except hers—at Johnson Elementary. The lesson that she seemed to be offering us was that if we were going to stand for anything worthwhile in our lives, then too often these would be our choices as well—and so we had better practice our church-building skills.

As I cross Harvard Yard, the noon bells chime and yellow banners summon my eyes again to the signs along the crosswalk:

CULTURES CROSSING

It is a calling to the senses, a calling for a new wakefulness among us—but how can we know the value of the summoning? From the brand of multiculturalism that we were learning in Room 20, I cannot help but think that we are going to need more than yellow signs—and we are going to need more than a month for this.

March, 1990

I have a breathtaking walk to share with you some day—from Herring Cove to Race Point. Even doing a few hundred feet is like sandpapering your soul. Just what the doctor ordered.

Until then,

D

KILLER BEES

Spring cleaning. I find a few stray tablets in my kitchen cabinet: coated for easy swallowing, with the labels CIBA 16 on them. Ritalin that other mothers left with me when they dropped off their boys to play with my son. Afternoon meds, as they called them, and which I seem to have forgotten to administer. I roll one of the tablets in the palm of my hand, and I see Sabrina Kaslov passing around a box of Junior Mints during arithmetic. "Something sweet to keep the wheels rolling," Miss D would say. I see two of The Busy People moving up and down our rows and collecting our chewed-up gum—one with a box of tissue and a recycled lunch bag for easy disposal, while the other one collects our morning compositions. In Room 20, we were always chewing and writing and moving and making and doing, and we had come to regard The Busy People as essential, even irreplaceable.

In the fifth grade, when Peter Hawkins repeatedly adjusted the window shades to our classroom when he should have been correcting his math problems, he would be chastised and banished to the miniature desk at the back of the room: "A first-grader's desk until you're ready for the fifth grade," our fifth-grade teacher muttered as she deposited Peter Hawkins in his new seat and squeezed his giant knees beneath its table.

But in the fourth grade, after several fanatical adjustments to our row of window shades so that each one lined up perfectly with the next—and in the end, a sliver of sunlight cut through the center of our classroom and split our rows into east and west banks—Miss D thanked Peter Hawkins out loud for this.

"At last, a cool climate to think in!" she exhaled gratefully, "Thank you, Peter."

As if equally satisfied with the atmosphere that he had created, Peter Hawkins eased into his chair in the west bank and bowed his head to the work on his desk. A few of us bent over our essays in the cool of this new shade, while others looked up from their pages and nodded at Peter Hawkins as if to offer their thanks as well. "Peter Hawkins," Miss D would announce to him on some of his more restless days, "No one works those shades like you do. I believe you will make a brilliant Signal Man on one of our navy ships!"

Conformity. Submission. Docility. These were what Miss D called the Killer Bees. "Don't get stung!" she would holler to us as we hurried down the corridor to recess, or as we shuffled off to our homes at the end of the day. The world, we had come to learn, was buzzing with Killer Bees—peers who would require our conformity; parents who would reward our submission; principals who would smile in approval at our docility. "We would have to dodge the bees," she used to say—and perhaps feel a different sting instead: the loneliness of the nonconformist, or the difficult-child label of the insubmissive, or the lashings of the principal's ire against a ten-year-old's transgressions.

I grab a paper towel to sweep up the tablets that are camouflaged in a dust of seasonings. Somewhere under a siege of spilled cumin and cardamom I find a tiny pink envelope. I think of all of the envelopes marked CONFIDENTIAL that the office would send up to our classroom and that would inevitably be deposited into Miss D's desk drawer, or sent back home at the end of the day.

"Mary Wiles," Miss D would announce, as she held up a small and serious envelope, "Your mother has sent you a decongestant! Shall we take a walk instead?"

And, before Mary Wiles could answer, The Busy People

would take the lead and we would thunder down the fire escape stairwell and out through the heavy red door, a door so thick and feudal that each time we pushed hard on that bar we felt sure an alarm would go off. But it never did. Once outside, the only sound we would hear was the rhythm of Miss D's exaggerated breathing:

"Hhhhhhhhh" and "Ahhhhhhhhhhhhhhhh!" and "Breathe, darlings!"

She would shout this command to us as if to make us conscious of a birthright that we were not exercising. And while we paraded around the playground, she would look back over the tops of our heads and wave her arms like a conductor:

"Breathe in! Huhhhhhhhhh."

"And out, Ahhhhhhhhhhh."

Bailey Arnold and a few of the boys would mock Miss D's exaggerated breathing by puffing up their chests and then letting them deflate. With each breath that they exhaled, they would round their small shoulders and then fall forward, tripping and knocking one another to the ground. The rest of us would follow Nicholas Kastinopoulos, who kept time with Miss D's breathing with his arms flying up and down. We slid over the icy playground and flapped and gasped like synchronized skaters.

"Okay, Mary darling?" Miss D would holler to Mary Wiles.

"Okay, Miss D darling," Mary Wiles would holler back playfully.

To the principal watching us from above, these were dubious calisthenics. To us, it was alternative medicine. Refreshed from our midmorning burst of cold air, and without the toll of a recess bell, we would fall back in line for our return. As The Busy People shepherded us up to the open landing of Camelot, we felt our skin warm to the building's warmth and we welcomed—in a way that we had not welcomed before— the contests inside.

October, 1991

Hold fast that which thou hast! That is my constant prayer for you.

Yours in battle,

D

VERITAS

She greets me at her front door with a hunched, half-pirouette that is meant to show me what she is wearing. "Hi, Teach," she says, with a wink. It is a tender reversal of roles: her addressing me this way to acknowledge my recent award, and her sporting the Harvard sweatshirt that I gave to her last time.

"It's you," I say to her absently, as if we are talking fashion, but, of course, it is not her at all. Nothing about this sweatshirt agrees with her, except possibly the emblem on the front: a Roman, wreathed tribute to truth with the Latin word broken into parts as if to summon meditation on its meaning: VE RI TAS.

Veritas. In the fourth grade, it was a concept personified. On a life-sized list of Roman gods and goddesses—a cast of names so long that it covered the door that joined our classroom to the classroom beside us—Veritas got special billing. While all of the other Roman gods on Miss D's giant list appeared alphabetically, Veritas held its place at the top of the list. As if to shake up this ancient pantheon of gods, or as if to create a new hierarchy of values, Miss D required that even Jupiter—god of all Roman gods—give up his throne and fall in line with all of the other gods whose names simply started with the letter *J.* Out with the swaggering sky god, who brandishes thunderbolts like ultimatums; in with the virginal goddess of honesty and truth. And in the myths that Miss D shared with us throughout the year, Veritas seemed to appear more often than the other gods—Veritas as mediator between deceitful gods; Veritas, as arbiter of right and wrong; Veritas, as a shield for the bearer of bad news.

Veritas vos liberabit! The truth will set you free! It was the refrain that Miss D and John G. Ashe took turns reading aloud one afternoon—a refrain that the brave Tiresias shouted at his own King Oedipus, a desperate and pathetic king who would not face the truth of his terrible life, and who would rather kill the messenger Tiresias than hear his message. "Veritas vos liberabit!" Miss D shouted in an exaggerated baritone, as she played the role of Tiresias in this mini drama of prophet against king, wisdom against arrogance, seer against blind man. And in a crescendo of solo and chorus, solo and chorus, she would cue John G. Ashe, who would leap to his feet to lead the rest of us:

"Veritas vos liberabit!" John G. Ashe shouted over our heads.

"Veritas vos liberabit!" we shouted back.

Among a pantheon of gods who struggled with the same human issues that we did—arrogance, jealousy, self-loathing—Veritas, the goddess of truth, came to be for us what she had been for the Romans: an absolute; a line in the sand; an end to debate; a bulletproof shield; a drink of cold water—and a virtue that, too often, we overlooked.

As if to assure us of our goodness in spite of our less than virtuous ways, or as if to respond to a question that only she had heard, Miss D suddenly halted us one morning in the middle of our arithmetic to make an announcement.

"Uh, darlings."

We looked up from our waterfalls of long division to hear what was on Miss D's mind.

"Did I tell you that Veritas, the goddess of truth, was so hard to find that it was believed by the Romans that she hid in the bottom of a holy well?"

And with this, Miss D shook her head as if she had amazed herself with her own story, and she returned to the work on her desk. It was only a matter of time before our trashcan became a holy well. "It's just what we need!" Sabrina Kaslov exclaimed, as if to say *problem solved.* And when it appeared that John G. Ashe or Nicholas Kastinopoulos or Bailey Arnold or Mary Wiles, or any one of us might be twisting the facts in our favor, Sabrina Kaslov would jump up from her seat and peer into the newly decorated and pristine trash can. "You sure it went that way?" she would ask the truth-bender, "cuz that's not what it says in this holy well."

When Sabrina Kaslov bowed her head into the holy well, she was not just playing the seer; she was judge and jury—arbiter of the truth. Inside the well were scraps of paper that others in our class had dropped there: notes that told anonymous testimonies, narratives that offered eyewitness accounts of what others in the class had seen or heard regarding issues large and small. As Sabrina peered into the well, she would reach for these scraps of paper and then read them aloud.

"It says here that Mary Wiles gave Bailey Arnold her favorite green-ink pen because she likes him."

"It says here that Bailey Arnold *stole* Mary Wiles's favorite green-ink pen."

"It says here that Mary Wiles is an Indian giver and she wants her favorite green-ink pen back because Bailey Arnold does not like her the way she likes him."

When Sabrina Kaslov seemed satisfied that we had achieved our goal, she would drop the testimonies back into the well and briskly brush her palms together as if to say *case closed,* or as if to wash her hands of something unpleasant. The rest of us would stay in our seats quietly reflecting on the testimonies that we had heard, and now and then glancing over at the one who had been incriminated—or else set free. We were not always sure which.

Truth as something drawn from a holy well. Truth as something elusive. Truth as personal testimony. Truth as an absolute that spares not even a fourth-grader. In Room 20, this was our introduction to the various ways of knowing things, an epistemology that would start with a trash-can-turned-holy-well to teach us how to distinguish between truth and falsehood, between right and wrong, between subjective and objective, between experience and essence.

It was our first dabbling with a branch of philosophy that, according to Miss D, made an elderly Plato question the very nature of his own reflection in a lake one sunny day. And when Miss D pointed to the bearded face above the blackboard a peculiar quiet fell over us as if we were imagining that lake, that reflection, that question. When Mary Wiles sighed that was sad about Plato, Miss D smiled and shook her head, "No, no, not sad at all—a very jolly old man," Miss D uttered, still pointing to the bearded face. And then dropping her arm and turning toward Mary as if to comfort her, Miss D sounded out the words, "A very happy man."

And so there was our open path: Miss D had watched us approvingly as we converted our classroom trashcan into a baroque-style holy well of truth, and now she would smile on us again as we turned our self-doubts into self-affirmations. From that day forward, questions about the nature of our own reflections would be life-affirming questions. From that day forward, the lessons of the holy well would be life-charging lessons that would carry us through grades five and six—and thereafter.

In Miss Diamond's fifth-grade class and in Mrs. Rogers's sixth-grade class, we would be easily distinguished from the others: We would be the ones raising our hands before the teacher asked a question—we had questions of our own. We would be the ones who thrilled at ambiguities—puzzles propelled us. We would be the ones who scoffed at standardized tests—rubrics could never reward our exceptional ideas. We would be the ones disrupting the politics of the playground—cliques could only foster a soul-killing conformity.

In the meantime, as the months turned into seasons in the fourth grade, we would consider that lake of Plato's now and then. By the time that Miss D pointed to the bearded face above our blackboard, we had become so at ease with metaphor that we understood that the lake that Plato peered into was not just a watering hole, but a mirror of sorts—a water world that reflected the nature of his existence, his essence. By deduction, we understood that our lakes, our mirrors, would reflect the nature of our existences. And so when Bailey Arnold taunted Sabrina Kaslov one day for primping her hair too conceitedly in front of an oval mirror that hung in the back of our classroom, Sabrina Kaslov pulled out all the stops—she called on metaphor and Plato all at once.

"Mirror, mirror, on the wall. Who's the most conceited of them all?" Bailey Arnold sang.

"Bailey Arnold is," Sabrina Kaslov snapped back.

And as she pulled him by the collar in front of the mirror, she added:

"See that puffed up nobody?"

When we saw our reflections in the window panels that ran along the wall of our classroom, we thought of Plato's lake. We saw a reflection of our lives in North Weymouth; we saw the likenesses between our profiles and our parents' profiles; we saw their vague impressions in our choices, our hopes, our essences. Unlike Plato, however, who could see only the divine in his lake reflection, we could not help but see something diabolical as well. And so, as the months turned into seasons in the fourth grade—seasons of unemployed fathers, seasons of mean-spirited teachers, seasons of playground bullies, seasons of belt marks on the back of a girl's legs—we would find ourselves looking into Miss D's beryl-blue eyes as if we were peering into that lake of Plato's.

We were looking for our mirror images in her eyes, looking for our essences in her essence, looking for answers that we were sure she could give us. In turn, Miss D would instruct us again and again to look into a different lake for answers—the lake that Plato saw, she would say, the lake inside your own heart, your own soul. Since metaphors made sense to us, her instruction did too. We would find our own lakes; we would look into our own hearts, our own souls. And as if on schedule in a curriculum of quantum leaps that Miss D had planned for us, we would find ourselves captivated by the suddenly self-reliant, suddenly embryonic, and exquisitely human images that we saw reflected there.

As if we are celebrating more than just a teaching award, it is sherry in good glasses today. Without offering me her usual choices—apple juice, ginger ale, or wine—she pours us each a glass of Taylor Tawny. When I click my glass against hers, she clicks back and then draws herself backwards and gasps as if she is suddenly seeing not only our raised glasses, but instead some panorama. I wonder if she sees what I see: I wonder if in this single instant, she sees the vista of our past two decades of friendship and the decade to come; as if all at once, the ten-year-old with pigtails in her fourth-grade class is a young woman; as if in the click of a glass, a vibrant fourth-grade teacher is an elderly woman with a monastic's hunched pose.

So much of our talk is like this: a gasp or a sigh from her that articulates a sudden intelligence; a back and forth of gestures that say more than themselves, mannerisms like memories that illuminate the past—and the present. It was a language that she incorporated into her fourth-grade curriculum and it is a language that works for us today—a body language, a talking in signs when talk alone seems inadequate.

In the fourth grade, when even this body language failed us—when Miss D seemed to need yet another tool to reach out to us—there were our classroom walls instead. All around us were mottos like ancient ideals that she had modernized for us by reproducing them in Crayola's newest colors: glittering silvers and golds. On the wall near the door to Exeter and covering the metal plaque that once said Fire Exit was instead a black poster board with gold cursive letters that seemed to warn us against a danger deadlier than fire:

TO THINE OWN SELF BE TRUE

On the door to our closet of art supplies, where we were accustomed to finding a list of rules for storing paint brushes and glue, was instead a slender note in silver crayon—*Know thyself*—a note that seemed to whisper to us some basic rule for artists. And on the wall above the blackboard at the front of the class, just below Plato's pouting face read the battle cry of the bearer of bad news:

VERITAS VOS LIBERABIT!

Like a shield of armor that we might draw down off the wall for our own use some day, this glittering and metallic banner would catch us in the eye some mornings as the shifting sun made its way across our classroom. Between lessons, or during lunch, or while waiting for the bell to ring, we would let our eyes pass over these mottos, these rallying cries. They would remind us of stories that they had been excerpted from, and we would wonder how they might fit into our stories—phrases like stage props for a life that we had not yet lived.

Instead of these maxims on her walls today, the face of her refrigerator has been transformed into a collage of credentials. Historically, it is the place where she posts welcome notices in plastic magnetic letters for her guests:

O HAPPY DAY!
HEIDI CAME TO STAY

Today, however, she has posted a whole story of sorts, a montage of photos and clippings in the shape of a wreath. And above the wreath, in plastic letters:

185

HEIDI'S LAUREL WREATH

On some of the laurel leaves are notes that she has scribbled, notes so faint and sinuous that they look like the veins of a vine, scribblings that chronicle high points in my life: Williams College! Such knowledge! ... Brown University Teaching Award! Good Lord! ... Radcliffe Fellowships! Hooray Hip Hip! ... Masters in Teaching! Now you're reaching! ... She has even included among my achievements my marriage and the birth of my first son. At the top of the wreath—as if to observe some zenith, some crowning touch—is the heading from a news clipping that I sent her:

Harvard's Danforth Prize for Teaching

"Don't worry, darling," she says as she catches me examining the laurel wreath, "lunch will be better than my artwork."

Her comment is just light enough to change the subject if we need to—a line that she is tossing out, as though she feels the same tectonic shift that I am suddenly feeling, as if to ride the shift with me and yet spare the both of us. I grab the line—although the best that I can do is to tell her that I love her artwork.

After lunch we try again. We talk and talk: Yeats and Yves Bonnefoy; the benefits of breastfeeding; the Gulf War; a peace rally that left her exhausted for days; the Irish; the Pope's condemnation of Ireland's IRA; Seamus Heaney's poetry; news about family and friends—and the Danforth Prize. It's Harvard's undergrads who do the nominating, I tell her in answer to her question. My students chose me.

"Uh-huh!"

In the fourth grade, this was always an exclamation that she reserved for dramatic effect: it meant *Bingo!* or *Voilà!* It was a prodding from her for us to see the importance of something that we had just said and to reflect on it.

"Uh-huh, darling!"

It was a push from her for us to make some connection,

to see some invisible matrix of life in front of us. In the end, it was always an invitation from her for us to see that matrix as some divination of our own lives, as some happy unfolding of a chain of events that we were somehow participating in. I am having trouble seeing what she sees. "Darling," she says leaning across the table toward me, "your students chose you. That's the best prize you can get." As if sensing my need for corroboration, she calls on Thoreau: "He could not be judged by a jury of his peers,"—and I finish the line for her—"because his peers did not exist!" It is a pas de deux that makes us laugh and that opens a path for more talk. I glance back at the laurel wreath the way that I used to glance up at the walls of her classroom whenever she called on me—looking for a place to start, looking for a prompt to say what I want to say, the truth that I want to tell her.

To thine own self be true. Veritas vos liberabit.

The truth that I want to tell her is that in spite of my recent accolades, I am certainly not the darling of all of my professors. I am not in a camp where camps seem so important.

"Well now, who are we?" she used to call out to us when we became tongue-tied during a poetry recitation, or when we found ourselves stuck in a math problem. "We are warriors!" Nicholas Kastinopoulos would typically shout out. "Problem solvers," Glen Rooney might respond in muffled tones from under his astronaut's helmet. "Beautiful," Sabrina Kaslov sighed for a response one day, "I'm beautiful."

To think harder about Miss D's question, there was a telescope in the back of our classroom that we took turns looking through. "Our observatory," Miss D called it, "to new worlds out there," she would say pointing to the sky— or, she would say, pointing to her head or to her heart, "to new worlds in here." Because we were allowed to visit the observatory whenever we wanted to—during math, in the middle of art class, at the start of composition—she expected a report from us. "Well, Captain?" she would whisper as she bent toward the occupied telescope, "Are we looking *outward* or *inward*?" The truth that I want to tell her is that I have gone to the observatory that would reveal new worlds to me and I have looked outward and I have looked inward. I have seen hallowed places, passages like tests of mettle or integrity—and I have seen the dark side of the moon.

As for the dark side of the moon, it has been—as she used to promise us—*a place where you make your own light.* The truth that I want to tell her is that during the past few years, I have had to make my own light—and I have felt its warmth and its unsettling exposure. As ageless as the gods are, Veritas has somehow aged. Although the list of gods and their virtues are the same, the guardians of truth have changed—and so we have looked down at our own feet and wondered if our positions, our convictions, our truths, must change as well.

"Still standing?" Miss D would ask us when we found ourselves facing the unexpected. "Quick! Check!" And like mimes confirming our own existences, we would clap our palms against our sides and down our trembling legs to confirm that we were indeed still standing. When we looked back up at her she would smile and bow. "Well, there's hope then," she would say. In the fourth grade, there were endless recognition ceremonies for those among us whom Miss D perceived as still standing, the ones whom she called Our Makers of Light—the ones who somehow turned bad into good, who turned difficulty into self-discovery, or who turned ostracism into opportunity.

For refusing to participate in recess during the week of her grandfather's death, Sabrina Kaslov would sit on the bench outside the principal's office five mornings in a row, while the rest of us filed by her in our march toward the playground's open field. Yet, at the end of the week, during an afternoon ceremony in our classroom that Bailey Arnold led off with a tune on his kazoo, Miss D awarded Sabrina Kaslov a gold medal. For every recess after that, Sabrina wore her gold medal like a badge of honor, as if her battle with the administrators of Johnson Elementary on earth had somehow assured the peaceful flight of her grandfather's soul toward heaven.

The Purple Heart that Miss D pinned to Tommy Breen's chest for slaying his dragon when he faced down the fifth-grade bullies—and Tommy Breen's promise that he would only remove the Purple Heart for baths—somehow encouraged the rest of us to become *dragon slayers* as well. These ceremonies and badges revealed the very nature of all the battles that we fought that year. All contests would inevitably become tests of character, tests of mettle—tests, as she used to say, "of the soles of our feet."

"Nothing like a good scuffle to know where we stand," she used to say to us, as she combed Tommy Breen's disheveled hair with her fingers and wiped his face clean with a tissue that Mary Wiles always offered, or a she brushed the dirt and leaves off of Nicholas Kastinopoulos's silk shirt, or as she clapped together the snowy sleeves of his jacket—recess after recess after recess.

When Nicholas Kastinopoulos was summoned by the office to apologize for one of his outbursts on the playground, Miss D's objection animated us: "Nicholas Kastinopoulos?" she called to him as he started to exit our classroom, "Who are you?" When he looked at her confused, she answered for him,

"You are a proud Greek boy who defended his dead father today."

Yes, Nicholas nodded his head.

Yes, some of the motherly girls nodded too.

"Are you going to apologize for that?" Miss D asked him.

No, he shook his head.

No, the majority of us agreed.

When Nicholas K. quietly resumed his place behind his desk, he seemed never more afraid of the consequences of fighting back, yet never more at peace with who he was.

For Miss D, our battles on the playground or our struggles with the authorities of Johnson Elementary were the very contests that showed us what we were made of. We were to understand these challenges as obstacles that would elicit from us strengths that we did not know we had, as opportunities to define ourselves.

"Our punishments will be our just rewards," she would assure Tommy Breen after a bout with the fifth-grade bullies, or as she kneeled in front of him after recess and propped him back up to his natural height.

Every contest is a passage, she seemed to be instructing us—and only a select few of us would come through intact. For those select few, there was a freestanding wooden frame, tall enough for Miss D to pass through with us in our ceremonies of passage. Nailed and hammered together by us and decorated in leaves and grass and flowers that we had gathered from the schoolyard, the wooden threshold wobbled as we struggled to hold it on each side and as the select few crossed through it. It was a ritual of passage, where our peers sang and cheered and threw bits of composition-paper-turned-confetti at the celebrant. We looked forward to the day when we would have our turn as well.

The coward or the conformist, we learned in Room 20, would not be among those who would have their turn—only those like Nicholas K. or Tommy Breen or Sabrina Kaslov, who stood for something larger than themselves and who had the scratches and bruises to prove it. "So lick your battle wounds and be happy," Miss D used to say to us. And we would. Suddenly puppies, we would lift up our paw-fists and slather our tongues across them—half of us ridiculing her life instructions for us, the other half rehearsing them.

༄

On the table between us—like a thrush opening its wings to the sun—are Yeats's collected poems; the open page worn from her hand gliding down it, other pages flagged for re-reading. "Read something, darling." It is another way that we talk, and so I find a page:

Turning and turning in the widening gyre
The falcon cannot hear the falconer;
Things fall apart; the centre cannot hold;
Mere anarchy is loosed upon the world,
The blood-dimmed tide is loosed, and everywhere
The ceremony of innocence is drowned;
The best lack all conviction, while the worst
Are full of passionate intensity.

She nods her head as if to say that, although I have finished reading, she is still listening. "The best lack all conviction," she repeats the line softly while still nodding her head. And then, as if to help me utter the thought that is lodged in my throat, "Well, convictions cause trouble, darling."

Yes, I nod in agreement.

When I hug her goodbye, I hear myself whisper a *thank you.* Because it's easier, I allow her to think that I am thanking her for lunch. But, of course that's not it. I am thankful that as I leave her embrace, I am seeing more clearly than ever the necessary trouble that convictions cause. I am thankful for her exclamations in the fourth grade that were prompts for us to look deeper, cues for us to see that invisible matrix that is the manifestation of one's being, one's core, one's essence. "Who are you?" she might have asked any one of us on that day when she stopped Nicholas Kastinopoulos. "Are you going to apologize for that?"

Know thyself. To thine own self be true. These were directives that seemed simple enough in the fourth grade, although when Sabrina Kaslov inquired about one of them, Miss D's answer might have given us more pause:

"What's that supposed to mean, anyways?" Sabrina Kaslov asked Miss D in a challenging tone. "How are you supposed to know if you are being true to yourself?"

"By the difficult days ahead of you," Miss D answered her soberly, "and by the trouble all around you."

As we draw apart from our goodbye embrace, she points to the emblem on her shirt. We laugh as if we are both enjoying the irony: Harvard's Veritas emblem will be our coat of arms today. "Veritas vos liberates," she whispers into my ear as she hugs me a second time. "Veritas," I say back. When I collect myself enough to utter the whole phrase it is so that I can say it like an article of faith—a covenant, not just between the two of us anymore but between me and my God, to say *yes* to the contests that define us, to dance through the difficult days, to take comfort in the troubles that lie ahead.

November, 1991

3 a.m.

It's dark, dark, dark outside. But full moon in my heart! Did I ever tell you my nickname at college was "Crack o' Dawn Kate"?

Yours,

D

What a Difference a Day Makes

The corridor floor seems over-waxed, as if anticipating royalty—barons and bishops, rather than the faculty and students who pace up and down this hall. I wonder if it is the slippery sheen that is slowing me down, or if it is the list of imperatives that I have waiting on my desk. Before I can decide, I am drawn to a colleague's open door by a soulful tune. On his radio, a song that at the age of ten I sang like a true believer. "What a Difference a Day Makes."

At Johnson Elementary in Room 20, it was what we sang for special occasions, and for no occasion at all. For the special occasions, birthdays or award days, we would roll the king's chair from Exeter into the center of the classroom, where the birthday celebrant or the prizewinner would sit, and we would launch into an a cappella production of our song: "What a Difference a Day Makes!"

For the rest of the day, Miss D would hum the song as she flitted around the classroom, sometimes shifting the beat into a jazzy and nasally production, and other times sounding it out with a more Classical murmur as she worked at her desk. Often, The Busy People would hum along with her as they bent over their lessons at their desks, until after a few minutes, a chorus of crooning would whir through our classroom like a Gregorian chant or a psalm.

But it was a song that we sang on uneventful days as well. As if on constant musical notice, we would happily comply with Miss D's biddings—on any given day—to stop what we were doing, to stop in our tracks, and to stand and sing.

On command—and by our own wills—we would rise to our feet in the middle of a quiet reading session, or put down our pencils at the start of a vocabulary quiz, or assemble ourselves in an open circle on our return from recess—and we would sing.

As unorthodox as this seemed to us, these interruptions from our lessons, these intermissions from descending ladders of long division, these sudden stops in the train of a story's plot, were always a welcome break. Sluggish and still heavy from our lessons, we would pull ourselves up from our desks and stretch and yawn exaggerated and yelping yawns. From his front-row desk, Bailey Arnold would turn toward us; he would raise his right conductor's arm until the rest of us, his choir, appeared ready. Sabrina Kaslov and the pretty girls would close our classroom door tight, but first they would look one last time down the long hallway outside of our classroom as if to catch sight of a potential trespasser or a killjoy.

When he sang, Glen Rooney would lift the shield of his astronaut's helmet; his thin, pale lips would tremble on certain consonants as if he had not had enough practice with them. By contrast, Nicholas Kastinopoulos would puff up his chest and exhale beautiful and fluent tenor tones. Bailey Arnold and The Busy People would bob their heads and dip and rock their shoulders to the beat of our song, while Miss D marched up and down our classroom rows, arms swinging, mouth singing, and drawing us all in. "What a difference a day makes!"

Now and then, Miss D would punch out a phrase with a swinging fist and she would bend toward one of us with a smile. When Miss D punched the air, we punched the air too. And when Miss D paused in her march, we paused in our song. From our desks, we would turn our heads to the student torward whom she leaned, and as she bent over the small head below her, we would start again—not simply singing this time, but bestowing a kind of communal blessing upon a peer.

In spite of its apparent foolishness, this was not a fool's paradise. The optimism that Miss D encouraged was not the sentimental optimism that Voltaire's professor recommended in his *Candide*. It was, plain and simple, a call to service: a call to live our lives, rather than surrender to them. What wore us down would now be what made us strong. Not hardships, but tests. Not optimism, but expectancy. When the girl with bruises looked back up at a hovering Miss D and silently mouthed the words to our song, we took that as a pledge to heal. When John Paul Ambrose III shifted his weight from one foot to the other while he stood with us in song, we took that as a pledge to choose a sobriety that he had not seen yet. When Tommy Breen stuttered and faltered only a few times on the letter D in the word *diff'rence*, we took that as a pledge to choose song over self-hatred. With a polyphony that drowned out his stops and starts, we carried Tommy Breen over his hurdles until, by the pitch of his voice, he seemed to be leading us instead.

In Room 20, a day made such a difference that we could barely keep up with the history that we were making. To make room for our achievements, the soberly titled Fire Drills and Safety Rules bulletin board was soon converted to a collage of student awards, news clippings, and birthday announcements. At the top of the board, instead of the old advice to STOP, LOOK, and LISTEN before entering crosswalks was a new instruction in black capital letters:

STAND BACK! WE'RE MAKING HISTORY!!

Tacked up next to John G. Ashe's First-Place Ribbon for Best Riddle was a newspaper photo of an artificial heart installed into the chest of a man. Side by side with Mary Gillis's Cubist Self-Portrait was the grainy, black-and-white photo of Neil Armstrong in the Gemini 8 spacecraft. Sharing a tack with Sabrina Kaslov's Penmanship Prize was a picture of The Beatles serenading a crush of swooning girls. Riddlers, heart surgeons; artists, astronauts; writers, musicians. Best riddle, best heart; first cubist self-portrait, first American dual launch; perfect penmanship, perfect songs. Johnson Public Elementary School, North Weymouth, Houston, Liverpool, earth, space, the universe. Our collage drew no lines between these places, no distinctions between news in Room 20 and news in the world—or in the universe.

Without these clear lines drawn, we began to forget clear distinctions that we had learned in our earlier grades: distinctions between the world and us, between old and young, between can and cannot, between doer and learner. Learning, in Room 20 was doing, and there was nothing stopping us now from achieving the glory and fame that the world was waiting for. Unlike our previous classrooms, Room 20 became a first-class laboratory—a conference for research, for discovery, for enlightenment, for great things, a haven for the heroic and for the historic—and before we could say no, a haven for us. And unlike later classrooms, this one would become as vibrant and alive as our most secret dreams.

Birthdays also shattered these lines, these learned distinctions. No matter whose birthday it was, it was a day of greatness. After a few rounds of "Happy Birthday to You," Miss D would toss her Magic Jacket over the shoulders of the birthday celebrant, and recite the names of all of the greats born on this day:

"John Paul Ambrose III. A great among greats! Born on the same day as Peter Il'yich Tchaikovsky, Russian composer; Louis IX, king of France; Marconi, inventor of the radio; Gladys L Presley, mother of Elvis; Ella Fitzgerald, jazz singer."

And on a bulletin board, under the gold-lettered heading, O HAPPY DAY, Miss D would post these famous names alongside ours. We would read our names intermingled with the names of these other glitterati until it was impossible to see ourselves separately. Although we knew it already, it surprised us to know again that czars and jazz singers and inventors once started their lives in the fourth grade—just as we did. We imagined these celebrities as young and unknown, and we envisioned ourselves as older—and immortal.

When the commoners were allowed to compete in the ancient Greek Olympics, Miss D once told us, it caught on. The common people loved the feel of laurel wreaths on their heads, of being hero for a day, but after a while they wanted that fame for more than a day. We came to know that want. Once invited in Room 20 to compete and triumph, we wanted that wreath again and again. In Room 20, one could earn fame for the usual things: for spelling bees, for poetry recitations, for math quizzes, for watercolors, for attendance. But one could also earn fame for less tangible things: for joining in, for pulling away, for saying yes, for saying no, for winning what could only be called a personal best. For these victories, Miss D would lead the award ceremony, since the nature of the award so often escaped even its recipient. Big Cheese, Heavyweight, Superstar, Summa Cum Laude, Mahatma, Major League, Ace!

Although we did not always understand the award, we loved the titles that Miss D gave to us, and we knew that we wanted this fame to last. And from the story of Greek democracy that we learned had started with the open Olympics, we knew that no worthwhile fame was ever handed over easily.

Although our days sounded themselves out in the shifts of a shipyard's horn, we could imagine now a different diurnal rhythm—a rhythm that, like the curling bands of flowers in a laurel wreath, we knew one day we would have to defend. And so for the time being, it was a rhythm that we tucked inside our hearts and kept to ourselves, and that we sang as a group on certain days in a happy, jazzy tune.

December, 1991

I understand exactly what you mean about composing in your head. But it's too easy. Everything sounds so much better than the written word, but all you get are floating ghosts. Don't stop writing on paper and at a desk—ever.

Lovingly,

D

DRAWER OF DEVOTIONS

As I tuck some papers into a desk drawer, I push back a column of crisp green files with hooks. For years, these files have stood at attention like good soldiers, hoping for labels and their own specialized contents. Lectures & Teaching Plans. Course Evaluations. Student Recommendations. Completed Writing. Works-in-Progress. The labels would be easy enough. For myself: teacher and writer. Or for Glen Rooney: bio-engineer and marathon runner perhaps. For Nicholas K.: historian and lover of red wines. What we became because of her influence. But the methods that she used to guide us here, the values, the shared life, the trajectory—these would surely be lost in neat files and labels.

When John G. Ashe complained one day that nothing in our fourth-grade classroom was filed accurately, and that the labels on our supplies boxes were all wrong—Paper Clips for the box that contained milk money, Pencils for the box of scissors—Miss D pointed to the bottom left drawer of her desk, and answered, *This* is our active file, darling. It was the file, the repository, the receptacle that she called our Drawer of Devotions. The bottom drawer in her classroom desk was stuffed to the brim, but not with the things that elementary-school teachers customarily take away from children: bubble gum, life-like rubber bugs, marbles of every type and color, balls and jacks, gossipy notes, the novice love letter of a ten-year-old. These were all safely tucked into our own desks, for our own use, in our own good time, and out of the principal's range.

The Drawer of Devotions was not filled with things taken away, but with things given away. Although it was her desk and her drawer, she called it ours because it was where we deposited our private thoughts and wishes: notes that she would encourage us to write and then drop into the drawer as if we were dropping them into a sacred box. Reflections or passing thoughts that we wanted to save by recording them.

"Thinkers never stop thinking," she would tell us, "and writers never stop writing. And what a tragedy to have to search for a forgotten thought—and what if that thought were the seed of the next great American novel! Oh, we can't have scattered seeds!" This last comment she would grumble at us, with her hands scattering invisible seeds, and her head slightly bowed and rocking from side to side, as if she were remembering some personal tragedy. We became sowers of seeds—at first, because we felt that we owed it to her; later, because we saw that we owed it to ourselves.

We came to love the loose sense of an assignment always hovering—the Drawer of Devotions always half open, expecting great ideas from us. When we approached Miss D for questions about our lessons, we would sometimes bang our shins on the open drawer. Rather than tend to our bruised shins, she would tend to the drawer to make sure that it had not closed shut. These notes, these devotions, were our relics in a stupa—our mantras—and she was as protective of them as our later teachers would be guardians of their own coats and handbags.

"Mr. Da Vinci had a notebook, and so will we," she told us, long before we knew who Da Vinci was. For many of us, it was our first notebook ever, and we received it with the excitement that comes with owning any new school supplies. After a while, the sound of someone tearing a page out of a notebook for the Drawer of Devotions would make us pause. "Great ideas sneak up on us!" Miss D had told us, "so we had better be ready for them." Whether it were in the middle of morning essays, or just before morning announcements, or during our precious lunch break, or in the midst of Miss D's parsing of Caesar's sentences on the blackboard, Miss D and the rest of us would momentarily stop what we were doing to acknowledge the page-tearer with a kind of reverence for thoughts recorded.

When the principal announced over the loudspeaker one morning that the coming week would be Great Ideas Week and that we were all invited to submit essays to a student competition, we felt a mix of excitement and alarm: excitement because we saw ourselves as champions of great ideas; alarm because apparently some people reserved only a week for this.

By midyear, Miss D had brought us a book filled with photos of Leonardo Da Vinci's notes: sketches of mechanical wings like helicopters; drawings of voluminous rivers flowing through tall mountains; a baby curled up inside its mother's womb, and a naked man who is the measure of all things. Curiosity after curiosity: What happens to boiling water? What makes the muscles contract? How does the birth canal open? We kept the book standing spread-eagle on its spine on one of our window ledges until we knew his drawings so well that we could find them with the flip of a finger.

We reveled in the liberty to record our own thoughts—not just during Great Ideas Week, but when the thoughts came to us. In the fourth grade, we were always brainstorming. In the fifth grade, on the other hand, Sabrina Kaslov would be sent to the principal's office for disrupting the lesson by tearing pages out of her notebook. When the teacher asked Sabrina to hand over her notes, Sabrina delivered her homework to the teacher, while she slipped her notes to Bailey Arnold. A few of us gasped with relief: Leonardo had written his notes in code, as if they too had been intended for a Drawer of

Devotions; surely Sabrina's notes were just as confidential, just as encoded, and surely they should not go from one hand to another in broad daylight, but should be tucked away for another later time, for good aging, for fermentation.

How could anyone expect Sabrina Kaslov to hand her notes over to her fifth-grade teacher as if they were evidence of a crime?

2

There were other things, besides our ideas and prayers and drawings in the Drawer of Devotions. There were Bailey Arnold's detention notices deposited and ignored; John Paul Ambrose III's pink tardy slips balled up and forgotten; Valentine cards from us to Miss D, with Hershey's Kisses and Sweet Tarts still clinging to them with their dry skeins of scotch tape. When the drawer began to catch on its own overflowing contents, we would empty our devotions into a large manila envelope and mail them off. We would make up an address and send them off with adequate postage—to nowhere and to everywhere—to 1200 Tic Tock Lane, USSR or to 2000 Ship Shape Shores, Ireland, or to more local addresses: 1,000 Weary Way, Quincy Fore River Shipyard, U.S.A. Before shipping our packages, Miss D would press stickers all over them reading:

FRAGILE
HANDLE WITH CARE

Stickers that seemed to offer directives not just to the postman, but also to the world in general. And in parentheses, at the bottom of the envelope, always the added note:

(LETTERS FROM THE FOURTH GRADE)

It was as if we were dropping our prayers into a running river for all the world to reach into and read. We pictured people finding the large envelope and bending over our ideas with a shared curiosity, or laughing deep belly laughs, or crying crystal jewel-shaped tears. The drawer seemed to overflow precisely when we wanted to send mail. Our bulging, stamped envelope was a message in a bottle, a trial balloon. It was what the Greeks called catharsis, what other traditions call a letting go. But, mostly it was a rehearsal in articulating our own ideas, a trial run in advancing our gifts and making contact with the world around us, a fourth-grade drill in making a difference—envelope after envelope, riverbank after riverbank after riverbank.

Her individuality so unconsciously assumed has made her popularity universal despite the austerity with which she judges herself. Her deft manipulation of words, her penchant for poetry, and her superb appreciation for all that is fine has more than proven its worth in her literary successes. Beneath her exquisite sense of the ridiculous and the humorous, one finds Caddy enthusiastic about your triumphs, brimming over with new ideas. The class of '32 rises and with a farewell toast wishes Caddy in return for her generosity and good-fellowship the nearest thing to a perfect life that anyone could have.

The Annales Yearbook, College of New Rochelle, Class of 1932

THE CLASS OF '32

The nearest thing to a perfect life that anyone could have. A favorite fourth-grade composition theme of Miss D's. In fact, when it came to moving beyond our composition pages and physically actualizing our near-perfect lives, Miss D's persistence astonished us. Many times, in just the fall semester alone, after we had sketched out in blue composition books the nearest thing to a perfect life that any one of us could imagine, Miss D would ask us to try the theme again as if to teach us not just the skill of revising, but the more compelling skill of reviving—reviving our dreams. And so, there were second drafts, third drafts, fourth, fifth. Each time we started a new draft, Miss D would write along with us. With a feverish energy, she would push her chalk across the blackboard openly composing in front of us as we quietly filled in the lines on our composition sheets.

Our drafts for our perfect lives were never quite freely composed, but instead were always plotted on exquisite timelines. In the same way that past points to present, so too, Miss D had told us, our present lives point to our perfect lives. And so, we would always start by using our crayons to trace an existing line in our composition books. We would deepen the line's color and broaden its width—a good, solid line for drawing up a good and solid life. Writing on top of these newly etched lines, we would track the maps of our lives from left to right: a few inches for the story of birth to the fourth grade, and the length of the remaining page for the dreamy stretch of present life to perfect life.

With a flourish that she always reserved for solving our

math problems or for drafting her perfect life, Sabrina Kaslov would draw her wooden ruler from its soft, plush sleeve and she would press the ruler hard against the light blue line in her book, while she dragged a red crayon across its straight edge. For a title to her drafts, in a rainbow of colored letters, she would write each time, The Unfinished Story of the Almost Perfect Life of Sabrina Kaslov.

Each time we flipped through our composition books to begin a new lesson, our timelines of our almost perfect lives would stand out from the other pages like nearly forgotten desires, like memories of a pulse that had once been palpable and true—and that, thankfully, we knew that we would return to in a fifth or sixth draft.

In Miss Diamond's fifth-grade class the following year, we abandoned our timelines and in effect, we stopped rehearsing for our almost perfect lives. We missed Miss D's feverish free-writing in a cloud of chalk and we begrudgingly forgot about Sabrina's fire-engine-red timeline that linked our present lives to our future lives—a lifeline that connected the rubrics of school to the scaffolding of our most private dreams.

As fifth graders, although we could not say exactly how, we knew that the learning objectives for us had narrowed. Doing well would require a shift of consciousness. It was a subtle shift, but for most of us by now it was a profound and fundamental shift: a turn from dreams that propelled us into a new world to goals that reflected—and even revered—our existing world. In the fifth grade, our new goals would look like natural outcomes: stories that we did not know yet but that were visible to us in our parents' eyes. Marriages and betrayals, child rearing and miscarriages, punch cards and time clocks, cookouts, funerals, weddings; it all seemed already inscribed into history. In the fifth grade, we seemed to concede that dreams were just that. The best place to plot your dreams, we quickly learned, was with the bookies from the

Shipyard; and when the Massachusetts Lottery brought *The Game* to our town, the dreamers were the men with meaty and rough hands, dirt under their fingernails and dressed like metalworkers, who cashed their checks and played their numbers at Smitty's Quick Mart.

In the fifth grade, the stories of our future lives seemed permanently suspended in the salty air that we breathed so easily but that newcomers to our town found damp and heavy. Sabrina Kaslov no longer trilled her sentences to us as we walked to school in the morning: she would not be an opera singer after all, but instead an expert palm reader like her grandmother. Nicholas Kastinopoulos no longer bothered us at recess with his calls for the Convening of Congress. His congress would be his brotherhood of uncles, longshore fishermen north of Boston whose hands seemed woven from the rope and leather and netting that was their work. Mary Wiles and the rest of us no longer paused before the palm reader's shop—our future lives were inscribed, not in the fortune teller's palm, but in the furrows of our father's foreheads. In this new claim on maturity—we were, after all, fifth-graders—we would adopt the worldview of our parents. By definition, this would be the worldview of the alcoholic whether or not we ever touched a drink: We would crave a routine in our lives that some might call a happy repetition; we would become champions of yearning, masters of mediocrity; we would want the anesthesia of weekends the way a junkie wants relief from his pain; we would marry our high school sweethearts the way the Greek gods married their siblings—in order to guarantee like-minded offspring.

Because our new goals seemed so apparent now, we knew that we had somehow surrendered our dreams. And yet, because of the imprint that our fourth-grade timelines had already made on our psyches, we knew that this could only be a temporary surrender. Surrendering without surrendering was, after all, something else that we had learned in the fourth grade. Often, it involved the politics of the playground: trading power for love. When, after a week of apparently unsanctioned friendliness toward a playground outcast, Linda Miles announced to her circle of pretty girls that the weird girl is a beautiful artist, it was as if she hoped that this would grant the weird girl a pass or at least grant Linda Miles readmission into her circle of pretties. "She's a weirdo," the second-in-command of all the pretty girls replied. "And so are you now!" But, in spite of this curse laid on her, Linda's face looked oddly relieved and bright.

Surrendering without surrendering meant going mum when Mrs. Rogers, the sixth-grade teacher, asked for names—and taking detention as a collective for the names that we would not say. "We will sit here," Miss D told us as we sat petrified in our seats while our peers filed out of the school building, free and homebound, "But we will sing." Surrendering without surrendering, we were learning in the fourth grade, meant handing over our beliefs—not to give them up, but rather to give them the light of day. "No good unless the light catches them," Miss D used to say to us. And so we stayed in our seats at two o'clock in the afternoon, but we did not write the expected sentences on the papers on our desks: I will speak to Mrs. Rogers when spoken to. I will speak to Mrs. Rogers when spoken to. I will speak....

We sang.

The timelines for her almost-perfect life that Miss D drew on the blackboard looked more like the electrocardiograms of a shockingly erratic heartbeat: solid flat lines that would suddenly pitch upward and then go flat again, and plateaus that would require steep descents before trailing off toward the unknown and nearest thing to a perfect life.

From the name of the street and the house that she drew on her timeline, we knew that Miss D lived in Weymouth, but we did not know that she lived with a sister named Ruth in a house overflowing with books and letters and guests. We could not imagine that the peaks and plateaus on her timeline were etchings from a life beyond our classroom. Peaks of political protests, plateaus of religious retreats; peaks of guests to cook for, letters to answer; classes to plan; plateaus of self-doubt, insomnia, and exhaustion.

As fourth-graders, we could not know then the degree to which our own illumination required her self-extinction. We could not know about the humanist orthodoxy behind her unorthodox methods. We could not know the depth of her forgiveness toward us; likewise, we could not know what her college classmates knew: the austerity with which she judges herself.

For the time being, it was enough for us to imagine from the importance that Miss D assigned to our every triumph and fear, that we somehow inhabited the perfect life that she had not yet drafted on the blackboard—that she had come to North Weymouth, to Johnson Public Elementary School, to our fourth-grade class, and into each of our lives in particular, in order to somehow make manifest her own perfect life.

July, 1992

I've been feeling kind of funny this summer. It's either the after-math of that spring pneumonia or a foretaste of senior citizen-ship. But, I promise you one thing—On the day you're here in Brewster, I'll feel just the way I useter!

So much love,

D

EMPHYSEMA

Em·phy-se·ma: a pathological condition of the lungs marked by an abnormal increase in the size of the air spaces, resulting in labored breathing and ...

I have the dictionary definition of her condition in front of me. I let my eyes pass over the terms until I begin to see things differently. It is as if I am laboring over a foreign translation. I look up for encouragement, but she is still sleeping. I copy the definition to a slip of paper on her desk that seems intended for this, and I tuck it into my coat pocket. *There is more than one way to know something,* she used to tell us, *start anywhere!*

I don't know where to start. I steady myself with some playacting: scanning the definition like an intern briefing myself with her medical chart. Instead, it is as if I am preparing for one of our science lessons—and since science was never a purely empirical subject in the fourth grade, I keep looking for the humanity in these terms.

"H-h-h-h-heidi," she whispers to me as she rouses from her sleep, "Under here...." I follow the wave of her hand to a box at the bottom of her nightstand. When I crouch down to reach for it, it is as if I am reaching into her classroom closet—a narrow, dark, and hallowed place.

Even as I bend over, I can hear her labored breathing. I think of the breath that she gave us: her gasps at our brilliance on Recitation Days. "Merrrrrrrhhhhhhhhh-cy," she would exclaim in the middle of our performances—and she would draw her palms-in-prayer to her chest as if she could not hold back her amazement. Instead of the staccato performance that might follow such sudden interruptions, a silky rhythm would give itself over to us like a river for us to swim in.

I think of her humming—that sonorous trail of music that made its way from her classroom to the east wing of Johnson Elementary each afternoon after recess, and that guided us back to her; a droning tune like the drumbeat of her pulse that helped us know when to start writing our compositions and when to stop. Start when she starts humming; stop when she stops humming. Her humming was the classical background music that scholars now know we need— fertilization for the soul when the mind is working hard.

I reach into the box and smooth my palm across a frayed thread near the hem, precisely where she used to tug it into a crooked pleat for Story Time. Tattered and resewn. Mythical patterns. Even here, it is less jacket than a costume for ceremony. The ceremony was story. We were her story.

I see the jacket loosely hung across her shoulders. "Ohhh-hhhh, Sabrina!!" she would suddenly call out as she read our morning compositions. "What a story you cooked up!" And just as we were settling back into our mazy math problems, "John G. Ashe! Such words! May I call you Cicero?"

This is a sit-in, this playing with thread. It is the passive resistance that she taught us to practice when life looks more like a machine. I tie the stray thread into a tiny bow, and I can barely hear the nurse asking me to leave.

KATHERINE DUNNING, 81 WAS WEYMOUTH SCHOOLTEACHER

Katherine Arthur Dunning, whose 37 years of unconventional teaching methods in the Weymouth elementary schools earned her a large and devoted host of lifelong admirers, died Sunday in her home in Brewster of emphysema. She was 81. Miss Dunning, known to her friends as Caddy, was born in Newark, N.J. She came to Weymouth at age 12 and lived there until 1974, when she retired to Brewster. She graduated from Sacred Heart High School in Weymouth and from the College of New Rochelle in New York. During her long service as a Weymouth teacher, Miss Dunning acquired a reputation as a creative and unorthodox teacher who tried to elicit each student's potential for achievement. She was a storyteller and liked to recite poetry to her classes. To add a dimension to the teaching of literature, for example, Miss Dunning would make a celebration out of observing the birthday of Robert Louis Stevenson, Nov. 13. As late as this year, Miss Dunning was receiving letters from former pupils, sometimes giving her credit for the shape the pupil's life has assumed and choice of such careers as professor of literature. Miss Dunning leaves a sister, Ruth Dunning of Brewster, three nieces, two nephews, and 13 grandnieces and grandnephews. A funeral Mass will be said at 11 a.m. Friday in Our Lady of the Cape Church in Brewster. Burial will be in Blue Hill Cemetery in Braintree.

The Boston Globe Newspaper,
December 9, 1992

November, 1992

We have kept so busy this Fall! I guess I'd rather have it this way. I will "not go gentle into that good night!"—that, you'll recognize, is a paraphrase of Dylan Thomas (wink).

Lovingly yours,

D

FOUR LAST THINGS

Death. Judgment. Heaven. Hell. The majority of us came into her classroom knowing these terms, these four last things; and, as a deep and worshiping Catholic, Katherine Arthur Dunning knew these terms too. Nevertheless, she lived according to a different catechism.

Not death, but life's breadth. Expectancy. Pilgrimage.
Not judgment, but a sinner's forgiveness. Grace. Caritas.
Not Hell, but a kind of husbandry. Deliverance. Advocacy.
Not Heaven after earth, but Heaven on earth.

When she spoke to us, when we spoke to her, she would bow and clasp her hands together as if to greet our divinity. Though a vibrant, middle-aged woman, her shoulders seemed eternally hunched in a way that, even as fourth-graders, we thought must have hurt her lungs, or her heart. It was a mendicant's posture, as if she were our roshi bending to our resistance, our innocence, our hopes and dreams—our beginner's minds. Teaching, we learned that year, was more than sweat and toil. It was life-giving.

We saw this giving of life in her raw finger tips when she applauded us, or in her disheveled blonde hair when she mimed the words from our spelling list, and in her lanky but dignified stride through the classroom with the blackboard's lesson impressed in chalk on the back of her navy blue dress: C I A O, which meant *Hello* in Italian—and which we learned during our lesson in A HUNDRED WAYS TO SAY HELLO. We knew that she would quiz us, and so we leaned our bodies to the left and then to the right one morning, so that we could copy the fading word off of the back of her dress while she briskly erased the blackboard. To check our class notes before the quiz, we would send her salutations in several languages at the top of the lessons that we turned in: *Ciao, Miss D! I hope you like my math quiz!!* And, as if to confirm our good spelling, she would answer us in our new native language: *Ciao, Nicholas!* and, *Bravo on your math quiz!!* The days were full of new and charming greetings: *Bon journo*, when we arrived in the morning, and *Salve*, when we returned from recess. And Bailey Arnold would often bow and theatrically shake Miss D's hand when he approached her:

Ciao, Signora D.

In the back of the classroom, one morning, an Italian opera sighed the word *Ciao* to the funereal rhythm of church bells. When John G. Ashe asked Miss D why the woman in the song sounded so sad every time she said "Hello," Miss D explained that in Italian *Ciao* means Hello *and* Goodbye. A few of us looked up from our composition papers to take that in. Sabrina Kaslov shook her head and slipped her No. 2 pencil back into its velvet sleeve, as if to say *lesson over*. And, as if to confide in the few of us who were still looking up from our lesson, Miss D placed her palms on her thighs and bent toward us: "Just hellos for now," she whispered to us, "Goodbyes will come soon enough."

ACKNOWLEDGMENTS

Heartfelt gratitude to contest judges and to the editors of the journals in which the following chapters previously appeared, sometimes in slightly different form:

Memoir (And), Summer 2008 for "Right Notes."
Memoir (And), Summer 2008 for "Isms."
Slippery Elm Literary Journal, 2015 for "A Purple Heart."
Chautauqua, June, 2016 for "Ex-Patriots."
The Carolina Quarterly, Summer 2016 for "The Good Thief."
Apeiron Review, Summer 2016 for "Fallen Angels."
Tulip Tree Publishing, 2018 for "A Good and Simple Meal."

The chapters "Right Notes" and "Isms" were recipients of the 2007 Penelope Niven Creative Nonfiction Award from Salem College, Emily Herring Wilson, Judge.

Information about the author can be found at:
www.mbmclatchey.com